Finding My Father's Faith

Finding My Father's Faith

Wynne Leon

Finding My Father's Faith
Wynne Leon

Wynne Leon
Seattle, WA

Copyright © 2015 by Wynne Leon. All rights reserved.
www.findingmyfathersfaith.com

No part of this publication may be reproduced or transmitted in any form or by any means, electronic, mechanical, including photocopying, or by any information storage and retrieval system without written permission from Wynne Leon except for the inclusion of brief quotations in a review.

All images, logos, quotes, and trademarks included in this book are subject to use according to trademark and copyright laws of the United States of America.

FIRST EDITION 2015

Leon, Wynne
Finding My Father's Faith
Wynne Leon

ISBN 978-1516803347
1. Memoir
2. Meditation
3. Religion

Book Design and Cover Design © 2015
Cover Design by Nick Zelinger
Book Design by Andrea Costantine
Editing by Carolyn Leon, Pam Kirby

All Rights Reserved by Wynne Leon

To my wonderful father for being a constant beacon to show me there is more depth to this life than meets the eye.

Introduction
November, 2014

THERE IS NOTHING LIKE A FUNERAL FOR A PASTOR. IT feels like a graduation ceremony for someone who has spent his whole life working towards the ultimate advanced degree. Over 1200 people came to celebrate Dad and more watched it livestream on the Internet—a large group that embodied a singular feeling. The atmosphere was joyful and everything about the service was so personal.

The tone was set by Mom, who architected the content and feeling of the service. Dad had prepared a document detailing the scripture and music he wanted at his funeral and had also preached a sermon on death just a few months before his accident so Mom had a good starting point. But more than content, it was her attitude that guided the services—first in Tucson and then in Bellevue—a gratefulness for Dad. Because she adopted this pose, instead of anger, drama or even frailty, everyone else was free to honor life, not focus on death. When I arrived at her home after the accident, it was clear that even amidst the shock, whether through faith, outlook or discipline, she was focused on the blessings she found. First, it was that her children were able to be with her in Tucson. Then as other friends joined us, it was for the blessing of the comfort of friends. But mostly it was for Dad. They were so close. On a weekend I spent with them when they had been married about 30 years, I awoke in the morning to hear them giggling together as they worked on a project and they giggled to the end, through 53 years of marriage. So, the spirit of the funeral was celebration and she created a true sense of Dad and his purpose in life.

The choir filed in, 150 strong with current members and past members returning to lift up the former pastor in song. This was enormous, after all this was a Presbyterian, not a Baptist, service. They were clad in maroon ankle-length robes and led by Scott Dean who worked alongside Dad for enough years to know how each piece delighted him. The robes reminded me of the black and grey robes that Dad wore throughout his career, billowing out behind him because he was always moving fast. He had a favorite story of the time during World-Wide Communion Sunday that he was positioned on a folding chair at the front of the church with guest pastors from around the world and as he sat, the chair flipped him backwards into the choir loft. Once he managed to right himself and stand, he quipped, "Now you all know that I do wear pants underneath my robe."

We sat in a sanctuary designed and built during his leadership and every element was one that he loved—the pipe organ, the stained glass, the shape, the peaked ceiling with a view of the sky. Dad once explained to me that Protestant theology is built for the ear and so the space of worship must be designed to facilitate hearing and understanding the gospel in a sermon, music or teaching.

This is opposed to cathedrals or places of worship designed for the eye to inspire a sense of awe. He wanted the space to create a sense of community and intimacy among the people and so it was as we gathered to applaud his vision and vitality.

The officiators, five of them, were a dream team of pastors and theologians, mentors, friends, successors, and the pastor's pastor. They knew him so well and they knew God. They formed a direct conduit of belief to carry him forward. There was no doubt about his theology or commitment to faith and so they were free to celebrate his journey forward. The Reverend Jeff Lincicome, pastor of the church Dad attended after his retirement, started it off, describing Dad as a "battery with feet, just looking for someone to jump start." Then Dr. Gary Demarest, Dad's mentor and college pastor who in part inspired Dad to ministry—with a voice, aptly described by my friend, like a redwood tree, if redwood trees could talk—launched us into the fulfillment of Dad's journey as he sonorously boomed 2 Timothy 4:7-8: "I have fought the good fight, I have finished the race, I have kept the faith. Now there is in store for me the crown of righteousness, which the Lord, the righteous Judge, will award to me on that day – and not only to me, but also to all who have longed for his appearing."

Dr. Dale Bruner, theologian and Biblical scholar, related a lifetime of stories, debates and encouragements as they kept the faith, first as friends at Princeton Seminary, then as couples when Kathy became Mom's best friend, then as families as they raised their sons, Fred and Michael, alongside us kids in the Philippines and Spokane, and finally as retired men of God who really never retired at all.

The Reverend Kendy Easley then took up the baton, describing Dad's faith not only in God but also in her as he recruited her husband Tyler fresh out of divinity school and in the process goaded her into ministry too. And finally, Dr. Scott Dudley, Dad's successor at Bellevue Presbyterian Church where we now sat, who with one vivid story skillfully told us of Dad as a mentor and friend and described Dad's character of humility and grace, and as the ultimate encourager.

My brother, Jay, and I were up next to eulogize Dad. It was an intimidating line-up to trail, but we had spent a life time following after a preeminent preacher so Dad had prepared us for this too. It seemed so important to me to bring him home as a father.

A pastor, my dad told me, has a role in the holiest moments in life, birth, death, baptism, marriage, crisis, and so it seemed that each person in attendance shared one or many of those holy moments in their life with Dad and came to witness his final holy moment. Some stories I knew because they came from the Williams, a second family to me; Dad performed the weddings for all three daughters and they'd all come—parents, daughters, husbands—from three states to honor him and support us. I heard many stories in the weeks after Dad's death: "Your dad helped me through the death of my father when I was just a teenager and so I came to honor him." And "Your dad inspired and encouraged my son into ministry." The repetition was a chorus, comforting and warm, "Your dad listened," "Your dad encouraged," "Your dad was my best friend," "Your dad stood with me in my time of grief."

In the summer of 2014, 13 years after my dad retired, he was very much alive at age 79 and his commitment to usefulness and service showed no sign of waning. He delivered over 26 talks (sermons at his home church, classes he taught, funerals, etc.). He also signed on to be chairman of the board of Kairos USA, an organization committed to peace in the Middle East. He was healthy, gregarious and active. Maybe too active.

Dad died in a bicycle accident in Tucson, Arizona on November 7, 2014. After spending a glorious morning on the patio in the sunshine reading his latest book, he left his long sleeve shirt on the back of the chair, his wedding ring, wallet and phone on his dresser and hopped on his bike. He was wearing his helmet and riding through the gated community in which he and Mom lived in the winter. Confidently riding three blocks from the house, he didn't stop at a stop sign, turned left and crashed into a car driven by a 19-year-old woman. According to the deputy sheriff that investigated the accident, Dad hit the front of the car head on and then flew up towards the windshield, hit the side post and then broke the passenger window and crumpled to the ground with a broken neck. The deputy said he was wearing shorts, a polo shirt and some kind of flannel shirt. But my dad didn't have any flannel shirts.

A few days after the accident, our family met Kaylee, the young woman who tried to perform CPR on Dad and held him when he died. Kaylee, 17 years old, was washing the windows in the back of her grandma's house and ran to Dad when she heard the accident. He wasn't ever conscious, was bleeding quite a bit and then died in about a minute or two without saying anything. Kaylee tried to stop the bleeding with the flannel shirt she was wearing.

In our conversation, Kaylee said she was trying to figure out her purpose in life. She thought that perhaps part of it was to be with Dad at that moment. Kaylee connected to him in that brief time before he passed and still felt a bond with him, as if he is her guardian angel. He was touching people's lives all the way to the very end and beyond. She came to the memorial service we had in Tucson, also magnificent and personal, led by Dr. Andy Ross, Dad's friend and pastor. In the guest book she entered, "Dear Mr. Leon, I met you at the end of your life but you have inspired me to continue mine."

When I got the call from Mom that Dad had died in a bike accident, I pictured it happening on one of the broad, busy streets in Tucson. But it was a quiet, barely traveled spot in their gated community that I've walked to a couple dozen times before and after the accident and seen no one. Standing at the corner, it's clear that his death was a kind of miracle, although not an easy one to accept. His life was a miracle and his death was a miracle, painless, quick and sudden, looking into the face of a beautiful young woman. He must have thought she was an angel and was probably trying to figure out her life story. He never had to endure growing old.

At the end of the Bellevue service, just before the bagpipes took up "Amazing Grace" and the choir joined in, the sun shone through the glass in the ceiling and there was a standing ovation for a life well lived and for a God who made such a man. The cheer and upwelling of admiration were palpable and so strong it almost pushed aside the grief. Dad was there in that light, and in his last holy moment encouraged us all to live that same spirit of service, encouragement, faith and love.

ONE
December 21, 2014

Dear Dad,

    I have some news. My plan was to tell you and Mom when you would be home for Christmas, but now I find myself writing the most long distance of all letters.

    I'm pregnant! Jay teases me because I myself am shocked at this news although I went to a fertility clinic, did all the preparation for in vitro fertilization, and then had an embryo implanted, so apparently I'm not supposed to be surprised. But that it worked the first time even though I was deep in grief over losing you, that I had finished all the paperwork and planning for it just one day before you died because otherwise I wouldn't have been able to finish the plan, that options of getting pregnant like this even exist for my generation and age, it all seems miraculous and so, yes, I am surprised. When I finished the paperwork on November 6, 2014, I sat for a few quiet minutes at my desk with the overwhelming sense that life was about to change. I had no inkling that the changes would start with *your accident the very next day, but this cycle of death and birth are intertwined in an unfathomable way for me even as I wish we were celebrating this together.*

The first question on the paperwork I filled out for the fertility clinic was, "Do you know why you haven't become pregnant before now? If yes, please explain." I filled in "Never tried." As you well know, I spent my twenties growing up and establishing my career, my thirties learning to climb mountains, spending my vacations climbing in Mexico, Russia or to Everest base camp, then getting married but not having kids, and my early forties figuring out how to move ahead with grace after divorce. Finally, there was no more time for dithering, it was now or never. A profile accompanies each potential sperm donor and the one I chose was tall, athletic, finishing his biology degree and going on to be a doctor and with a good family health history. But what caught my eye was the section on personality questions. The donors rate personality characteristics and on the optimistic – pessimistic scale, he marked himself and his entire family down as optimists. Now that should fit well with our family!

Of course, as with any major change, I'm scared, especially as a single mom. I don't know if you heard Jay's eulogy, but he says that many of his fatherly responses come directly from you, from things that you said when we were growing up, and that those responses are pretty darn wise. I can only hope I will have that same instinct. The last time I saw you, I told you that you always made me feel so special and loved. I will do my absolute best to pass that feeling down to my child.

All the materials we were working on in the couple years before your death—the recordings of your stories, your writings and emails you sent me, as well as your comments on the draft of my project—are infinitely more important to me now. I want to keep asking you questions to find out how you led your life through faith, how faith shaped you, and to work with you to discover the pieces that are passed between generations and the ones each child must make their own. But I know that you have already given me the answers, and it is up to me now to weave them together into my own story. I am so lucky that we were finally able to have all those conversations that brought us together despite our different spiritual practices, helping me to see how faith adds a depth to life and family. I wish for my child, as you wished for me, that deep contentment that comes from faith and know, as you did, that the expression of faith will likely differ in this next generation. I have so much in addition to your example to accompany me on my path forward, but I feel such a weight of responsibility for doing it well. I want to pass on the legacy of all that you were—the fun, the laughter, the faith in God and in the best of people, the joyfulness, and the love and delight in others. I know by now you are wanting to deflect all my admiration of you, giving credit to God and turning it around in a way to encourage me. You always despised arrogance in any form, but Dad, you defined a life well lived, loving and encouraging so many others.

Please know that the family is taking such good care of me in this time. Mom in her delight and willingness to be useful as always and Jay and Lindsey in their enthusiasm and optimism about what the future will bring. We all miss you so much, but in the wake of your death and this new life coming into the family we are figuring out the roles to support each other. And when I am most fretful about whether I can do this, I feel you from just beyond the curtain, as you once described it to me, nudging me with your elbow, laughing, pulling me in close with your twinkling brown eyes and encouraging me. You live on through us and in this new life to come.

I love you, Dad, the best of all Dads!
W

TWO

I THINK OF A RECORDING FROM 1972 OF US AS CHILdren when we were living in the Philippines. As we packed to move to the Philippines in late 1969, American troop involvement in Vietnam was at its peak. Ferdinand Marcos had just been reelected President in an election noted for its violence and voter fraud. According to the Wikipedia article on Marcos, he used $56 million from the government treasury to fund the campaign and had almost bankrupted the country. There was a growing anti-American spirit among young people especially, kids that had not grown up with a deep affection for America for saving the Philippines from the Japanese. Mom and Dad felt deeply that moving to the Philippines for Dad to take on his second pastorate, the Union Church of Manila, was God's calling and so there is no sense of concern on the tape from my mom or any of the kids. Because of the intense heat and humidity, we often gathered as a family in one room and turned up the air-conditioner. So, Mom has brought us together to make a tape to send back to her parents in the States. She has everything organized, she is calm and prepared and so too are her kids, waiting for our different turns to talk.

Jay, age nine, captivated by a boat (a ketch, he said) that he recently saw at the Manila Yacht Club sailing to Hong Kong, describes with great awe the big-ness of it, the sails, the ropes, the crew, at one point saying that the ropes themselves must have weighed at least two tons. Already at nine, he has an air of authority and leadership about him.

I'm only three so there is clearly nothing on my mind when it is my turn, I can't compete with the vision of my brother so I seem to try some good-natured patter of show and tell in front of the audio mike, bringing over items in the room and telling what they are. "In this tainer" I say, gently corrected by my mom, "con-tainer," "in this con-tainer is water but in this container is Kentucky Fried Chicken!" At which point Jay says, "That is nothing but soap and water!" I continue the happy patter as if the details are no matter.

My first memories come from those six years in the Philippines, some of the best years for being together as a family. There were fewer weddings and funerals for my dad to officiate because the church largely served the ex-patriot community who travelled home for those events. We had no television and instead had places to go like the Polo Club where my brother practiced his swimming for swim team, my parents played tennis and I mostly got sunburned, despite the hats, long sleeve shirts and sunscreen. We had live-in help, a cook and a cleaning person who could also watch the children, as well as additional help with laundry, driving and gardening, so it eased the domestic chores, freeing up Mom especially to pursue her independent nature, putting on piano recitals and studying Russian.

Mom recounted some of the allure of the Philippines. "One thing that was neat about our years in the Philippines was that Manila was similar to New York City, Washington DC, LA, Chicago, Hollywood – everything in America put together in one place. So, that's why we got to see Mohammed Ali fight Joe Frazier (The Thrilla in Manilla, October, 1975), and we were nearly in the front row when Van Cliburn performed at the Cultural Center (July, 1973). I remember seeing Bobby Fischer at the Polo Club. And the Pope's visit in November 1970. It's where everything happened, right there." Even though martial law was declared in late 1972, everybody still came to this country under military rule.

We are all there on that recording, already stepping into the people we become. Jay, all vision and big dreams, will become an entrepreneur, awfully good at turning ideas into big eventualities. I, a happy little putterer, will become an engineer and computer consultant, good at problem-solving. Mom is there, smart, capable, and kind, able to keep us all together. Dad, though not present for the recording, is evident in all of us. Jay gets his humor and ability to see the whole picture and I get the good-natured, let's-get-it-done character. But it appears none of us inherit the faith part.

Dad's faith, integrated with my mom's in marriage, was so formed and solid by the time of these first memories that it covered us like an invisible mantle. At 43, I finally wanted to make that mantle visible and I had barely two years to talk with him about it before he died.

Early in 2014, after spending about nine months gathering writings from Dad, interviewing him and Mom about their stories, and sorting this all into a very rough written draft, I wanted to let the rest of the family know what we had been doing. There wasn't an event that I could identify as to why we didn't talk about faith in our family now; it was just the way that it had been ever since we became adults. We were required to go to church until a certain age and then free to make our own decisions. And, we had decided not to.

I prepared my pitch. "So, I've been talking to Dad about his life and his career in a way that we never seem to discuss. I think we need to come to terms with faith in our family and sooner is better than later while Mom and Dad are still living, so I've written about 80 pages that I'd love to have you read to the degree you are interested."

It was hard to open that can of worms. We had great relationships with Dad without talking about religion and were not likely to agree, especially if we got down to the details. Jay was interested and supportive and so that helped propel me forward into these dangerous waters.

Even without a memorable disagreement with Dad about religion, I still have a lump of resistance to the church in me. Looking back now, I see how the church played more of a bogey-man role in my young life as the entity that would judge my father's performance based on my behavior. It was also the church with whom I competed for my dad's time and attention and was the measuring stick for new friends. While the church community has helped my parents select and nurture many wonderful friendships with fantastic people through whom I benefitted mightily in my life growing up and beyond, it seemed unfair to me as a selection criteria to predict a child's goodness based on whether or not their parents went to church. Amongst the kids in high school that I naturally gravitated towards, smart and happy, it seemed to me that the parental church affiliation didn't have any bearing on whether a kid would experiment with drugs or alcohol, be unruly or have a bad attitude. Not that they were more likely but neither were they less likely.

So, I didn't find the truth or comfort in the church that my dad did. I didn't rebel hard against it, just found myself falling away from it in college.

In doing some soul-searching, I read Dr. M. Scott Peck's book *Further Along the Road Less Traveled*, and in it he describes four stages of faith. The first stage, chaotic/antisocial, he reserves for people with anti-social tendencies; his second stage is formal/institutional in which faith is governed by an outside body, typically the church. I was mesmerized by his description of children raised by people of the church; it was like reading a description of my childhood, so good that maybe it was too good. He wrote:

> What happens to a child raised in such a stable, loving home and treated with dignity and importance? That child will absorb his parents' religious principles – be they Christian, Buddhist, Muslim, or Jewish – like mother's milk. By the time the child reaches adolescence, these principles will have become virtually engraved on his heart or "internalized," to use the psychiatric term. But once this happens, they will no longer need to depend upon an institution for their governance. It is at this time, which in healthy human development is usually at adolescence, that they start saying, "Who needs these silly myths and superstitions and this fuddy-duddy old institution?" They will then begin—often to their parents' utterly unnecessary horror and chagrin—to fall away from the church, having become doubters or agnostics or atheists. At this point they have begun to convert to Stage Three, which I call "skeptic/individual."

Dr. Peck then describes these stage-three people as usually scientific, truth-seeking people who often begin to see patterns in the big picture that tie them back to the beliefs of their parents and when they do, they transition to stage four, mystical/communal, "people who have seen a kind of cohesion beneath the surface of things." He goes on to relate the stages to religions:

> Indeed, one of the things that characterize all of the world's great religions is that they seem to have a capacity to speak to people in both Stage Two and Stage Four as if the very teachings of a given religion have two different translations. To take an example from Judaism, Psalm 111 ends with "The fear of the Lord is the beginning of wisdom." At Stage Two this is translated to mean, "When you start fearing that big cop in the sky, you really wise up." That's true. At Stage Four it is translated to mean, "The awe of God shows you the way to enlightenment." And that is also true.

I also had a more personal issue with the church. When I think of a pastor, I think of someone who preaches, yet I know from experience that is just one of the jobs a pastor does. Dad's pattern was to spend Monday focused on church administration with the full-time staff, Tuesday, Wednesday, and Thursday mornings working on his sermons or other writings for speeches or meetings, and then the afternoons of those days in one-on-one meetings or counseling sessions with church members. Monday–Thursday nights he would come home for dinner and then head back to the church for meetings, such as session, finance, planning, or mission committees. He would take Friday off unless he was doing a wedding or wedding rehearsal. Saturday afternoons he would mostly take off unless there was a wedding or funeral, and then he'd preach at several services on Sunday. If someone was sick or had died, often he'd squeeze in a hospital visit or a home visit with the family. God and God's work were hard to compete with, especially as a kid.

Fortunately for both my dad and me, my mom was very present and did the majority of the parenting when we were growing up. Early in my college years, Dad walked in on a conversation Mom and I were having and asked me a specific question. I had a particularly petulant moment and growled, "Dad, you don't just get to be a level 10 friend without doing all the work to get there." But it was impossible to stay angry with Dad. He was always there at the important times, like the piano recital or the tennis match, he was always positive and open, and he meant so well. The fact was that he loved his work and was very good at it. I was missing the point in my childish peevishness.

So whether I was a stage three skeptic or nursing a childish God-grudge, I didn't think much about faith or spirituality until my path in life became messy and I stumbled into a spiritual practice of my own.

THREE

MY FIRST MEDIATION CLASS TOOK PLACE A WEEK BEfore my divorce. We had been separated for two years, had no children, gone to a mediator, split all our assets and filed with the courts so it was not an occasion for which any remaining action was involved. It wasn't easy to say exactly how I felt, but I missed being me, the cheery, energetic, optimistic self I had been before the trouble. I felt coagulated somehow, stuck.

I was on the mailing list for my friend, Deirdre's, upcoming classes. I didn't know anything about meditation, but the class description spoke to me:

> "**DROP IN**/FIND SOME PEACE—cultivate internal quiet through low-key movements, breath practices and guided meditations to create sanctuary during these stressful times. Perfect for this time of year. "

All the words individually made sense, but together? Breath practices to create sanctuary? Still maybe the class could help me unstick the coagulated me. My brain fizzed out but my heart signed up and then my hands paid $25.

It was from 8:45am-10am on a Tuesday morning. I left the class and cried for the rest of the morning. Not a sob, it was more of a relatively peaceful, steady, cleansing stream which called for sunglasses while walking my dog on a cloudy October morning in Seattle so as not to alarm others. While I had spent a lot of time leading up to the divorce feeding some pretty righteous justification, after the meditation class I felt the space in me open for the grief of the regrets and failings for my part in the marriage. It was as if dead, stinky pockets of grief and regret I didn't realize I was carrying with me were finally aerated. It was a first step in getting past myself, yet I hadn't taken that step in almost three years of struggle because I had so much grist in the mill.

The trouble came on December 30, 2008. I was 39 years old. One of my business partners had invited me to lunch at Jalisco's, a small Mexican restaurant in northeast Seattle. We had never had a meeting without our third partner, but he asked and I went. When we walked in, he asked for a table away from the other occupied tables in a section that was not open and ordered me a beer. In my memory, his hands were shaking and that struck me as false, but it could well have been my hands that were shaking. I haven't seen a lot of horror movies but enough that I was just getting the feeling that I was walking into a shed with all the chain saws when he told me about my husband's infidelities. But he wasn't just my husband, he was our third business partner.

And so I learned the details of my husband's infidelities, of the weekend in 2007 that he spent with one of our clients at a wine tasting function, all of it witnessed by my business partner and my business partner's girlfriend, who also happened to be an employee of our company because apparently we couldn't keep anything separate. And a weekend in 2006 that my husband spent with my partner's sister, whom he'd flown down to California to be with him during a golf academy trip that I had given him for Christmas.

My partner had a solution to the problem though. If I fired my husband, he and I could run our small high-tech company of 19 together. I never was good at unraveling my partner's motivations and completely unable to even think straight at that moment, but I don't think this was his motivation for telling me. I think he told me because my husband had forced him to fire his girlfriend and this was payback, conscious or not. I didn't want to run the company with this partner. It had been my company before I was married and had morphed into this partnership over time. My partner was my husband's addition because they were friends, at least they once were. My husband and my partner were quite good at what they did so it was a lucrative partnership. But it was also stressful, a hot bed of personnel problems with 19 very unique and talented characters with a skillset that was highly in demand, never marching in a row. It wasn't paradise shattered by the news but it was an intricately woven web.

I didn't fire my husband nor did we separate right away. Instead we sold off the division of the company that my partner led at a fire sale rate and tried to work on the rest. We were completely at odds; I felt betrayed by my husband and my husband felt betrayed by our partner. We went to counseling. After ten months, I said I couldn't do it anymore and he moved out.

So, I had much grist for the mill. I probably could stoke up many more years' worth and was doing a fantastic job of that—

until the meditation class. There was nothing specific in the class to do with relationships or heartbreak, although the teacher, my good friend, Deirdre, knew well that I was sitting in a morass. It simply was breathing as a way to find sanctuary and it felt like my spirit was ready to run with it. I had a small glimpse of a way to get unstuck and it felt right. Not a miracle cure of my old habits, from which I would skip back and forth for some time to come, but it called to me to start.

I began to admit that I was not happy in the marriage long before learning of the infidelities but couldn't take the blame of being the one to say so; that I like to focus on the positive and so haven't developed a comfort for communicating the negative; that I avoid conflict and in doing so avoid sharing my feelings in a real way that could make a difference; that I had a very real spiritual side that was withering with inattention.

Opening also allowed me to really take a look at my Dad, who, 76 at the time, was so joyful and energetic and becoming more so. Dad was all that is good with this world—a man who sparkled with goodness and light. A person who lived his faith but allowed me my own path, someone full of energy and confidence, fun and funny, who made me want to be a better person just by being in his company. In fact, that was one of his unique gifts, the ability to listen and encourage. Somehow he managed to have the energy to do it in almost every interaction he had, whether he knew the person or not. It was a spark, a jolt, a passing of joy and he maintained enough juice to pass it on to everyone. In the absence of my joy, I wanted to learn where his came from.

FOUR

WHEN I ARRIVED AT THAT FIRST MEDITATION CLASS, I had no concept that meditation would become a spiritual practice for me or that I would even attend the class more than once. It was held in Deirdre's office, a quiet, intimate space usually used for massage, about 12' by 16', with three women whom I didn't know, plus Deirdre, whom I had known for about 15 years. Yoga mats were laid out on the floor with bean-filled cushions (bolsters, as I found out they are called) and a wool blanket. Deirdre explained that we sat on the bolsters so that our hips were higher than our knees, a more comfortable position for long periods of sitting still so we wouldn't be distracted by physical discomfort. As soon as she said that, I thought I would never make it for an hour and fifteen minutes. I was already experiencing mental anguish at the thought of doing no perceivable activity for that long, but I consoled myself with a long list of things I had done that surely were harder than that. Then Deirdre rang the chimes and we were off. She led us through some breathing exercises (inhaling, counting the number of beats for the inhale, exhaling, counting the number of beats for the exhale and repeating, eventually lengthening the number of beats), light yoga, and auditory exercises (listening to a piece of music and following the instrument playing the melody through the whole song). The idea was to give the mind something focused to do so that it wouldn't be off running through what was for lunch, the to-do list, or the latest conversation with a co-worker. I was terrible at it! My mind felt like a dog in a yard full of squirrels chasing one gray, fuzzy thought after another and so I was genuinely surprised when I felt the impact at the end of class. I felt renewed and calmed, ready to let go of old stories and face the uneasiness that I felt within, that internal dissatisfaction with the level of life I was living and an inkling that I needed to learn something before I moved on to the next relationship or phase of life. But even feeling those things felt different from other times that I knew I needed a change, like a cool, calm acceptance instead of five-point plan with an agenda and schedule. I signed up for the next class and when the email came for the next month's class offerings, I eagerly looked for the meditation class, hoping it was something Deirdre would continue to offer. I wasn't any better at it, but I was hooked.

The good thing about failure is that it offers the opportunity to challenge assumptions. Not that I want to be any better acquainted with failure, but when my marriage failed, I was free to take a good look at my underpinnings. I had plenty of assumptions that could use examination, minor alteration and perhaps major rework: that hard work can solve anything; that suffering in life is to be avoided; that belief in God means going to a Presbyterian church; that a spiritual life was defined by the way Mom and Dad did it; that God exists but has no part in my daily life.

To satisfy the orderly side of my brain, I needed to know how meditation worked so I started reading. In just scratching the surface, I found many types of meditation, schools of thought, and practices, but the commonality seemed to be breathing. Pema Chödrön, a Buddhist nun, describes that this is because breath is impermanent.

> It's always changing; it's always flowing; it's not a stable thing. By focusing on the breath, you're feeling something rather than concentrating on something. And you're also developing your mind, training your mind, to be able to stay present to the impermanence of things—impermanence of thoughts, impermanence of emotions, impermanence of sights and sounds, all the things that don't stay stable.

That's how it felt for me, feeling something rather than concentrating on something.

Pema Chödrön became one of my favorite authors on Buddhist philosophy and meditation. I liked the Buddhists because they talked so openly about suffering and corrected the assumption I believed for too long—that one could avoid suffering. The Buddhist teachings on how to lean in to suffering so as not to ignore it, extend it, or be sickened by all the methods I used to avoid it gave me so much peace and allowed me to stop struggling. In addition to weekly meditation class, I meditated daily on my own following a book, *The Book of Awakening* by Mark Nepo that draws from all sorts of traditions—Christian, Jewish, Hindi, Shinto, Native American, and his own poetry and that of others—and soon I had a spiritual practice that was different from my parents but worked for me. The universality and newness appealed to me and so I was more open to learn. I learned to sit down for ten minutes in the morning and read the day's meditation – a quote, a longer explanation and then some suggestions on how to meditate on it. I got something out of it every day whether or not the topic of the day was relevant to me—either inspiration, education or just a few minutes of calm. Whether I was feeling rushed, satisfied, joyful, lonely, grumbly, tired, it was a reminder that life was bigger than my own small window on the world. Mark Nepo has a fabulous way of illustrating a theme like perspective: imagine how a chick feels at the moment its shell breaks, the whole world it has known has come to an end. He touches on faith as the ability to know that the sun will shine even if you can't see it behind the clouds. Renewal is a theme that he comes back to many times, succinctly pointing out, "The culmination of one love, one dream, one self is the anonymous seed of the next." He defines courage: "Despite all consequence, there is an inevitable honoring of what is true, and at this deep level of inner voice, it is not a summoning of will, but a following of true knowing."

I had three years from the time I started meditating to the time Dad died. I spent the first nine months sticking with our status quo and not talking about spirituality. Part of the problem was that Dad and I were stuck in a mutual admiration loop, a genuinely happy relationship. We bonded over doing projects together, liked to laugh and joke so we had a light-hearted ease. I'd been freed by my divorce to redefine myself independently, yet I still had the same relationship with my parents. I was a result of a stage two family of faith as Dr. Peck described it, treated with dignity and importance and I returned that respect for my parents and who they were. There was no doubt about what their beliefs had done for them. They were happy, had fabulous and supportive friends, were dedicated to and active in being useful to others, and were so emotionally and spiritually healthy that I certainly couldn't argue the results. They weren't going to change, nor did I want them to, so it felt pointless.

But then a package showed up in the mail one day. Dad dared to challenge the unwritten family rule by giving me a book, *Know Doubt* by John Ortberg, and included a letter:

> I have wrestled with giving you this book and writing this note for a couple of weeks and have finally given in and decided to risk it. In one sense this seems a bit odd for this to feel risky. But given our respective personalities and our penchant for avoiding stress, it feels that way to me. I think we both skirt around the topic of faith on the notion that we are in such different places it would only add tension between us. But, for me, there is nothing more important in life than this issue of faith and I love you so much I can't just let this book gift pass without giving it a try.
>
> The thing that lies behind this for me is a long struggle with some really big doubts in my life and faith that I don't talk about with anyone. And so this book by a guy I respect very much has been a huge gift to me. He puts into words a lot of things that I have come to with this struggle and he has helped me believe that my faith-choices-in-spite-of-my-doubts are the right choices to have made and this has helped me cope better with lingering doubts. For example, his treatment of the whole issue of "uncertainty" was really remarkable and helpful to me and very insightful.

And as I read the book there were countless times that I thought of you. For example, his talk of three kinds of convictions and the deepest being our 'core convictions' made me think of you. I think you have more faith-stuff in you than you let on and this book might be a help to you in that way too.

One other thought makes it seem right to pass this book to you at this time. I have seen so many people in my ministry going through times of deep change in their lives and it seems that those are also times of deep thought and reflection that have been creative and good for them. You are in the middle of a lot of change these days. There must be some serious disappointment that your marriage has not worked out as you had dreamed and intended. Your life has been the story of one big success after another and you don't have many things in your life that don't work out well and so this time must be unsettling. So just maybe this time of change is also a time when you are questioning and thinking about big stuff like faith and doubt and your life-view. If so, I really think this little book might be a good read for you. At least I hope so.

Either way, Wynne, I love you very much regardless of where you are on these important matters of faith and doubt and life-view. There is nothing that you can do to weaken that love and this book is only a small gift that I hope will be a helpful and timely read.

I love you,
Dad

I read the book, but it was the letter that really mattered. Dad's point dovetailed perfectly with what I was reading at the time, Pema Chödrön's *When Things Fall Apart*. I knew I was in the thick of change when that was the title recommended to me! The point came home to me that having a conversation about spirituality, regardless of whether we agreed on the details, was about the real intimacy that comes from meaningful topics, the meat of life as Dad would call it. Passing up on the opportunity to talk with Dad now that I had some perspective and had lived more than a little bit of life was something I could no longer do. Dad was cheering me on and opening the door, giving me confidence and energy along the way. My parents did a great job of instilling confidence in their kids, Dad with his whole-hearted gusto and belief in us and Mom with her ability to break down goals into actionable chunks. From an early age they instilled the belief that I could do anything I set my mind to but also emphasized that discipline and hard work were my responsibility to bring to the table. They lived that way.

When I decided to study electrical engineering in college, Mom and Dad didn't ask how many girls were part of that program but instead treated it as an opportunity to troop down to see that part of the UW campus that they didn't really know from their years at the U. After I took up amateur mountain climbing in my 30's, Mom and Dad enthusiastically hiked with me up to 10,000 feet on Mt. Rainier instead of suggesting I should be doing something else with my free time. When I decided to start my own business, they didn't ask how many businesses fail in the first five years but instead read the technical books that I published. It worked even when I tried for things that weren't good fits for me like drill team in junior high. I can't find a beat even if it's bagged and tagged but they let me try out if I'd do the practice. It worked,

I practiced, they applauded the practice and by the second year I tried, I made the team (back row, middle). They were truthful in their praise so they used positive reinforcement to gently find my strengths, sometimes in comedic ways. Dad's goaded me into goodness in many pursuits. Playing tennis with him, he came to the net and dared me to hit the passing shot, hitting it right back to me if I didn't quite get it, laughing the whole time. When golfing, Dad's commentary ran along the lines of, "Wow, you hit that so straight! Straight into the trees." Or "Goodness, you really got a piece of that one. Too bad that water hazard was in the way." And then, when I hit into the rough, Dad was the first one over to help me find my ball.

This confidence and belief in hard work gave me the latitude to be independent. Then Dad rejoiced in that independence. If he privately thought I was doing things the hard way, he never said. But Dad had that independence as well, charting his own path when he was just a teenager.

FIVE

IN MY 20'S, MY JOB IN THE FAMILY WAS TO PICK UP Nana, my dad's mom, and drive her to family functions because she and I lived only a couple of miles apart. Nana was always up to something interesting all the way until the day she died at age 89. Nana was so proud of her son and all he'd accomplished. They were both very alike in their confidence, sociability and good-naturedness. She was a good storyteller, keeping me entertained for the drive, usually about 15-20 minutes each way. Sometimes she told about being up until midnight shelving books in the retirement community library because she was President of the library association. Other times, she related stories about growing up and the family. It was on one of these trips that she told me a story I had never heard before about how she dedicated Dad to God. For me, the mystery was why it was a secret.

My grandmother, Helen, and grandfather, Doug, met in high school where she was a year behind him. A rebel, Doug never finished high school and instead went to work at Washington Title Insurance Co, where he spent almost all of his working years, starting as a file boy and working his way up to Vice President by the time he retired.

Helen and Doug married in 1929, had Margie in 1934 and Dad in 1935. While they were very loving and supportive parents, there were elements of his childhood that Dad was determined not to perpetuate. His recollection was that:

> My dad always came home and had a drink, with Mom, and that led to his being what I've called a 'gentle alcoholic.' I have some bad memories of times he drank too much. He was a complex guy. Very loving, gentle, kind, hardworking and wanting to be supportive of anything I did. But there was very little 'serious talk' around the family, nothing about feelings or being vulnerable, and Dad especially avoided conflict to the point of leaving the room when something hot came up.
>
> I think my dad always felt inadequate, perhaps from being poorly educated among college graduates who were his peers. Socially, however, he was personable, upbeat and had a great sense of humor. Everyone knew him, he was a hard worker and when people came to the title company, they would ask for Doug because he was their friend. Many people later on in my life would comment, "Oh, I knew your dad, he was one of the greatest guys." He wasn't much of a reader or a deep thinker, but he got along with everyone and mastered

the skills of the company. I worked at the title insurance company one summer and could see firsthand that he was a very well-respected guy.

Helen was the youngest child of a Norwegian family that had moved from Minnesota to Seattle the year before she was born in 1910. Her parents were Lutheran, being Norwegian, and her father was very strict about religion; as it turned out none of the thirteen kids had much to do with the church as adults. Doug's mother was Episcopalian, and because of her influence, Doug and Helen had their kids baptized in the Episcopal Church, but that was the extent of their church involvement. To my mind, given this background, the prayer Nana told me about was quite extraordinary.

I never talked with anyone about Nana's prayer until I started working with Dad on this project, twenty years or so later when Dad was 77.

Following his birth on March 9, 1935, at Providence Hospital in Seattle, Washington, Dad contracted dysentery at the hospital and was sickly for two years, eventually resulting in rickets. Finally, at the end of his second year, Nana was exhausted and worried. One day out in the back yard in the weak Seattle sun, trying to get him to soak up some Vitamin D, she made a bargain with God that if He would save him, my dad would be HIS for a life time.

Dad's sister, Margie, older by 11 months, filled in a few more details. All 13 bottle-fed babies born the same week as Dad contracted dysentery because the machine for sterilizing the bottles was contaminated. Dad was the only baby to survive. She also added one more dimension about her mom's "secret:" "She was a very distraught mother at that time, and Dick did get better after that... so she was sure her offer to God was heard and she didn't tell anyone about this at the time."

From early on, Dad had a hunger for his life to be useful. When I asked about activities in high school, it was no surprise, given his energy and enthusiasm in his seventies, that his answer was, "In high school I was into everything. I was President of the band, also President of the Student Council, Captain of the swim team (I'd turned out for basketball but was a flop), Senior Editor of the Newspaper, Vice President of the Boys Club, President of the Sophomore Class ... bunches of stuff."

The summer of 1951, when Dad was 16, Billy Graham came to Seattle and held revival meetings for five weeks. According to a *Seattle Times* article on September 3, 1951, covering the last night of his five-week preaching, 443,500 people attended his campaign held in the High School Memorial Stadium and 6,841 made "Decisions for Christ." My dad was one of those decisions.

Dad went to hear Billy Graham with his friend Eddie Rutledge and Eddie's parents, who were like second parents to him, and two other friends. The four guys were bored and broke and decided it seemed like a good plan to go to the revival.

At that time Billy Graham was a 32-year-old preacher and the accounts of his preaching have an odd political feel now given our remove from the cold war times. The *Seattle Times* on Aug 13, 1951 reported:

> He waved his arms, crouched, occasionally thrust an accusing finger at the crowd, and spoke in a resounding voice as he delivered what is perhaps his best-known sermon. Mr. Graham studded his sermon with comparisons of the times of Daniel with the present world troubles. "If God would allow a pagan nation like Babylon to destroy his chosen country of Israel in an-

cient times, he could use the force of the Russian Army to drive America to her knees and to God. I believe that God is giving our nation one more chance to turn to the faith of our fathers. I believe that America can yet be saved from judgment that is surely coming if we get down on our knees and repent our sins."

Dad's recollection of the message that night was:

> Billy Graham emphasized that only one thing is sure, certain and true and that is the person of Jesus Christ. The issue of His being true is what has stuck with me ever since. I decided that if I had any integrity I had to follow this person of Truth until I found out otherwise. We had sat high up in the stands thinking we'd have a better view of the show, but when I raised my hand to indicate his message had struck me deeply and was asked to come down to the stadium floor (I never thought that was part of the evening), it was one long trek. To my surprise it turned out all four of us guys ended up coming down.

As strong as his faith turned out to be in directing his life, Dad's natural ability as a leader also played a large part in how his life unfolded. When I asked him about discovering that talent, he said:

> It was always a surprise to be chosen. I remember one time when I went to a Boy Scout camp at Camp Orkila on Orcas Island. Bill Hagen was also there, he was my hero, a great guy, basketball player, baseball player, all everything.

> After several days there, they choose people to be in the red scarf club. I can still remember this because I thought 'Bill is certainly going to get that' and he did. Then I did too and I thought, "What did I do? I didn't do anything! How'd that happen?" It was always kind of a surprise when things like that happened.

Dad's conversion to Christianity endorsed his hunger to be useful. He joined Mount Baker Park Presbyterian Church and the pastor became a life-long friend.

His conversion gave him the substance and meaning that was missing from home. His hunger for usefulness had a focused aim and the conversion, according to Dad, "connected me to the church and gave me a set of values and a sense of meaning in life, really, that God had something to do with who I was and what I was going to do. But I had no notion of ministry at that time. No one in our family had been around the church, let alone had been a pastor, so that would have been weird, that would have been really strange." His mom had not yet told him of her prayer. When I asked Dad about this, he said that Nana did finally tell him when he was almost finished with seminary. He thought that the story was interesting but he was a firm believer in free will. It seemed to me he was saying that he made his own choice.

SIX

I REMEMBER CLEARLY THE MOMENT I OPENED UP TO talking with Dad about faith and spirituality. Mom and Dad and I were walking with my golden retriever, Biscuit, up three flights of shaded concrete stairs. We emerged from the covering of dense trees into the bright sunlight of a small cul-de-sac and the scene couldn't have been a more perfect metaphor for a door opening. In that moment, I stopped needing to know the answers, pretending that I was any less flawed than I am. I didn't need to be afraid of the past or the future but instead I could simply be authentic. I had confused discernment with sophistication and thought safe conversation was getting along and in so doing had limited my experience to what was observably real. The richness and vibrancy of my father that was always present now flowed into me in a way that I was ready to feel.

This is also the moment that I became a seeker, looking for truths bigger than I had previously perceived. While I felt vulnerable opening up to listen and learn, as if doing so threatened the fixed membrane of what protected me, it also seemed the only way to grow. As meditation became my way of aerating the stinky pockets of stale emotions and ideas, openness became my way of trying to ensure my spirit stayed fresh.

Mark Nepo reveals the secret to openness in *The Book of Awakening*.

> Such a simple secret: by letting things out, we also let things in. So if you're cut off, in pain, estranged, numb – sing, give voice to anything. In needn't sound pretty. Simple, bravely open despite the difficulty, and let what is in out, and what is out in. Sing, and your life will continue.

I had needlessly worried that talking about all this important, heavy meaningful stuff would mean that we wouldn't be having fun.

Dad had an entrance script when he came to my house that was so familiar I could set a clock to it. He'd knock twice, open the door, gather me in a big hug, say "Great to see you" and then "Where is that super pup?" He'd go outside with Biscuit who knew his part in this script and had already picked out his toy. Dad would throw the toy until Biscuit lay down and then come back inside and say with gusto, "Let's get to work." His energy was so infectious that I could just surf in his wake and be carried along on his compliments. "Wow, look at all the great preparation you've done!" We continued to bond over our projects.

In the summer of 2012, the project was to redo the slate tiling on the concrete walls on the side of my driveway. We had tiled the walls six summers previously, but the weather had taken a toll on the most exposed sections. So even with this project that was completely cosmetic, silly when we first did it, and then even sillier that we were redoing parts of it, Dad thought it would be a ton of fun. He thought every project sounded like a ton of fun, except for plumbing but those projects were okay too. Mom and Dad showed up with their work clothes, their constant sunny attitudes, and enthusiasm.

Dad cut each custom tile, taking the measurement with me, walking over to the table we had set the wet saw on, marking the tile exactingly, kneeling down on one knee to make the cut and then walking the cut tile over. We started a call and response on the measurements so that "1 ½ by 2" became a chant we repeated until that tile was done so that we were having fun, talking and laughing while not forgetting. "This is going to be the best looking driveway in the county!" he'd intersperse. We went on for at least eight hours, with a short break for lunch. "Fantastic lunch! You treat the workers awfully well. Now let's get back to work."

By the end of the day, Dad was saturated with the blowback from the wet saw. The only clean spot around his eyes was under the safety glasses. Mom set the tiles, adjusting the spacers and cleaning each tile. It was the detail jobs she always did with her steadfastness and quieter strength, saving Dad and me from the messes that would be no fun to clean up, always present but not so vocal. Dad mixed every bucket of cement and Mom continually replaced our cleaning rags and water.

"We just want to be useful," my parents said. A handle, as my brother, Jay, calls it. Dad had a way of coming up with a handle for ideas so that you could carry them with you. Being useful was one of those handles, code for seeing what someone else needs done from their point of view, getting it done and not crowing about how helpful you are so that you eat up all the emotional credit. Dad was genuinely happy when being useful, bringing a lot of joy to every project, so before I'd know it, I'd be singing with him "right side up is upside down" when cutting crown molding or giggling as he mudded my hand along with the dry wall as we went along. "This is going to be great, kid."

I shared a personality trait with Dad, a need to finish things. It's an anxiety I feel in the center of my chest that grows until I finish something. It could be as simple as typing up meeting notes immediately after a meeting to be done with it. As soon as I think it, I have to do it; it's just not worth fighting. It almost feels rooted in superstition--if I know I should do something but then I don't do it, I will deserve the outcome whether it be a customer complaint, an appliance that fails or a mess I have to clean up at an inconvenient time and it'll be doubly bad because I KNEW I should have done it. I feel that way about this manuscript—I have to finish it as soon as possible because Dad entrusted me with the material and although I feel good at this time in my pregnancy, what if I don't feel well later and then I'll regret it.

Dad shared this restlessness--he cleaned the grill before bringing in the meat, or when I fixed a turkey for Thanksgiving, he would nearly wrestle the roasting pan out of my hands before I could get the scrapings out in order to wash it. He was funny and light-hearted about it but persistent, always pushing to go faster and get things done. When I bought my first house, I wanted to take down the wood paneling and dry wall my bedroom. We bought the materials and Dad taught me how to hang the dry wall sections. The wall was 8'3" tall and the dry wall only 8' high so we worked out that we'd hang it flush with the ceiling and then cover the gap at the bottom with molding. We put up the first two sections together and then Dad had to leave. But before he left, he built me a 3" platform to place the dry wall on while I set the screws. He understood too well that there was no way I could wait until he could return before hanging the rest.

In the fall of 2011, my parents organized a small group to put on dinner for homeless teens in the University district of Seattle. They committed to a night and then the team planned, prepared and served all the food with some instruction from the full-time staff. Each of us on the team had signed up for different items – the turkey burger sliders, buns, condiments, salad, baked beans, three different kinds of brownies, and so on. On the day of the event, a Saturday, my dad was having stomach pain, thought it was his appendix, and went to the emergency room where he was told it would be at least a three hour wait. He left. We worked all evening, unloading the food from the cars, preparing it in the kitchen, standing the whole time, then rolling it on carts from the kitchen to the room in which it was served. Dad was his usual self, energetic, the fastest worker, and encourager-in-chief, "That looks great!" He must have been hurting but there was no indication from watching him.

Although Dad was retired, he was too busy on Sunday to deal with whatever was causing the pain so he waited until Monday morning to see his regular doctor. Appendicitis was the immediate diagnosis. Dad once again tried to delay the appendectomy because he had things to do but found that his doctor had already checked him into the hospital. Fortunately, the appendix had not yet burst.

So, I understood that Dad suffered some anxiety about whether he had done enough. He liked his work and was very well intentioned but he also was driven. This feeling served him in many ways; it made him work incredibly hard, but it led to my biggest question – what part does God play? I saw a man of faith working hard, heard from everyone around me what a wonderful, important man he was, and equated the working hard to success. I didn't witness Dad leaving anything up to "faith" to get done or even relying on faith to avoid a bad outcome. So, what does one have faith in? What do you need faith for? What does faith feel like?

We spent that summer having fun and doing projects but also having a new depth to our conversations about traditions and how to live honorable lives. One morning in the fall, shortly after Mom and Dad had left for their winter escape in Tucson, I was meditating. The house was quiet, my eyes were closed, I could just start to feel the sun coming in through the windows and got this strong sense that I needed to write something about Dad. This totally disrupted the mood, my eyes flew open and my head kicked in to tell me all the reasons it was stupid: I wasn't a writer, I didn't have enough religiosity to be able to understand, and I had other things to do like running my own business. I tried to just let the thought arise like a bubble to the surface of water, just witness it go by and move on as I had been taught. I shut my eyes again and tried to go back to a calm state without an agenda. I gave up after five minutes as I just couldn't shake the feeling. There were a few items I could count in the pro column: I had spent 40+ years observing Dad, I had plenty of experience not following his example to provide contrast, and I was willing to try. The worst I could do, I figured, would be to learn more from him and have the opportunity to lavish some attention on him after a lifetime of just soaking up all he had given me. I hoped the content would flow from the same source as the idea right onto the paper. Except for a one page description of what I hoped to write, it didn't happen so quickly, but Dad did go along with my idea.

I was genuinely interested in his body of work, of which he has so much, since he delivered about 1600 sermons in his career, in addition to his doctoral thesis and numerous speaking engagements. I was also wanting to answer my question about what part faith played in his persona. I wanted to define what role faith has in daily life. He valued discipline, giving, being of service to others, and moderation in food and drink (he didn't drink alcohol at all). This focused him on the spiritual instead of the material, humility instead of power, forgiveness instead of revenge, and created a spiritually and physically healthy, graceful, and peaceful life. In just living by his attitudes, disciplines and values, he was on the road to good health, harmony with others, and a lifetime of working hard by doing good. This left me wondering where faith entered the equation in the balance and joyfulness of his life. Perhaps it isn't possible for one person to know that about another, but I figured there was no better person with whom to try.

In *Indiana Jones and the Last Crusade*, Indiana's dad, an archeologist like Indiana, goes missing and Indiana receives his Grail diary in the mail. He resents his father's forty-year quest to find the Holy Grail because it was an obsession that often eclipsed his being a father. The diary is the result of his dad's lifelong work including a map with no names and riddles about how to survive the final three tests to get the Grail. Indiana needs to solve the three riddles to retrieve the Grail and save his father's life and the last test involves faith, stepping out across a chasm where it appears there is no path.

Dad sent me a small sampling of his writing, ten devotions he'd written for a monthly publication put out by his church in Tucson, Northminster Presbyterian, and three sermons. The devotions were about a page long, centered on a verse or two from the Bible, accompanied by some insights about the text for the reader to ponder and use to guide their prayers. While I had heard Dad speak many times, it was great to have a small collection to pore over and study his work on paper. Then in the summer of 2013, I recorded our conversations as Mom, Dad and I would meet on Saturdays, go for a walk and talk about the stories, philosophies and influences of his life.

I hesitated to call that inclination to write about Dad, or even the timing of it given Dad's death, a Divine inspiration because I had not yet really begun to accept how the patterns of life are more mysterious than I could imagine, but in hindsight it was clear that mystery was already at work. What astonishes me was how open Dad was to hearing Divine inspiration because he was so young and inexperienced when he felt his calling to become a pastor and decided to test it out.

SEVEN

What Makes Us Great? by Rev. Dr. Dick Leon,
Daily Devotions, June 2011, Volume 38, No. 6,
Northminster Presbyterian Church, Tucson, AZ

Jesus said to them, "The kings of the Gentiles lord it over them; and those who exercise authority over them call themselves Benefactors. But you are not to be like that. Instead, the greatest among you should be like the youngest, and the one who rules like the one who serves." Luke 22:25-26

ENTERING THE UNIVERSITY OF WASHINGTON (UW) IN the fall of 1953, my dad pledged the Alpha Delta Phi fraternity. Right away the house chose him to run for freshman class president. The Alpha Delts knew how to run a campaign. In a big field of about 15 candidates, Dad ran as "Moby Dick" – with a big white whale on the signs in the Quad on campus. In Dad's recollection, he nosed in with a win by seven or eight votes.

Dad attended the University Presbyterian Church (UPC) and Calvin Club for college aged kids. Gary Demarest was the college pastor and as former Cal Berkeley student body president, baseball team member, and graduate of Fuller Seminary's first class, Gary was an engaging and accomplished mentor. Dad credited Gary for much of his involvement in UPC during those years, which I don't doubt given the depth of friendship they shared for all the years after. Dad said,

> Much of my sense of call into ministry started with Gary. At that time he was organizing campus leaders to speak at 'Chapter Nights' at fraternities and sororities. It was a bit daunting for me but he asked me to be one of them along with two senior heroes of the campus, the captain of the basketball team, Mike McCutcheon, and the president of the Women's Association, Lou Clark. Every Monday night we went to a different house and gave our testimonies. That meant a lot to me. I was doing something significant, helping people think through big questions, and that really had a lot to do with my ultimate choice of going into ministry. It was more a response to an inner compulsion from God that I had to follow if I was honest with myself.

During Dad's freshman year while serving as a counselor at a high school conference for UPC, he first felt called into the ministry. During one of the breaks, Dad was praying and heard a voice in his head say, "You should go into the ministry." At the time he laughed it off wondering, "Where in the world did that idea come from? This is really crazy." He had no family role model in ministry, no history, no connection at all. He thought the idea would fade, but after a couple of months he still couldn't shake it so he talked with Gary about what it meant. Gary was very encouraging but advised him to go slowly on pursuing it to make sure it was right. So Dad didn't tell anybody else about this thought for two years. Finally at the end of his sophomore year, he decided to spend the summer testing out this sense of calling. Dad was chosen as one of five guys to serve on a Deputation Team to work with Wycliffe Bible Translators in Peru.

When Dad recalled this mission, he lit up, delight animating his features.

> It was the first 'foreign' summer deputation team from University Presbyterian Church. To cut expenses Gary put us on a Greyhound bus to Miami and then on TAN airlines that took twice as long to fly to Lima as the other airlines. I didn't know much about church life, pastors or missionaries. I perceived missionaries as people who had left society and gone to work with primitive people in the jungle. They probably were a bunch of losers because they couldn't make it anywhere else. Well, I ended up being so impressed! The missionaries were the brightest, most devoted, honorable, winsome, talented people I'd ever met. These men and women move into a primitive tribe that has no written language, listen to their sounds, create a vocabulary and an alphabet, and THEN translate the Bible into their language. Their task is huge, and these missionaries are brilliant!

According to Wikipedia, TAN Airlines (Transportes Aereos Nacionales SA) was a Honduran airline " . . . formed in 1947 by private investors to operate cargo flights by contract. By 1950, the company started scheduled passenger and cargo services. By March 1960, the fleet consisted of three C-46's serving a route network that was 1,180 miles (1,900 km) long." It's not hard to imagine how an airline originally designed to fly cargo with only three planes took twice as long to get to South America. When Gary came to Seattle to speak at Dad's funeral, I asked him about these transportation arrangements. He told me that he managed to send two teams instead of one on that budget by using the bus/cargo airline and at 89 years of age, Gary was still chuckling about it!

It was the power of transformation that Dad witnessed that summer, not only in himself as he further committed to his path but also in some of the tribes that adopted new faith. His favorite was Tariri, a tribal chief converted by the Wycliffe Bible Translators, an amusing and engaging man by all accounts.

In Peru we spent the first three weeks in the capital Lima. Also called the Summer Institute of Linguistics (SIL), Wycliffe was celebrating its 10-year anniversary of work in Peru. So, they flew Tariri, who had ridden only in canoes, in from the jungle in a float plane to the jungle base, then from the jungle base to an airport and a commercial flight over the Andes Mountains to Lima. When he rode in cars, he would roll the windows up and down in wonder of it all. He had never sat at a table, never used silverware, never had eaten the kind of food we ate. He was wiry, short, and always colder than the dickens because it was so much hotter in the jungle. They gave him a suit with rolled up pants and sleeves because they couldn't find anything that would fit him. By the end of his first meal he was so dexterous that just by watching everybody he could use the silverware. One of the funniest stories, retold by the missionaries back in the jungle who lived adjacent to his tent, was about the food. When asked how it was, he said, "It was terrible, terrible!" "Well, did you get sick?" and he said, "I couldn't get sick, their floors were too nice!"

He was on the cover of the paper almost every day. When they took him down to see a big ocean liner, he exclaimed, "Wow, you have such a big canoe." He put on a demonstration for the Anniversary celebration by showing us how to use a blow gun. He would practice at a distance of about 25 feet aiming at a board with a drawing of a bird. He held the 6-foot-long blow gun with both hands near the mouth, elbows out and <pfff-tt>, the arrow would go every time right into the neck of the bird. All the homes in that area had high walls around them. The neighbor kids knew he was there and would peep over the wall, their heads coming up all around the top of the wall to watch him practice. He would shoot a couple of times at the target, then he'd get a little smirk on his face and would load up the blow gun, draw it up and aim it at the top of the wall and all the heads would quickly drop down. Then he'd laugh and laugh at his little trick.

There is a book about him called *Tariri* that tells how his tribe used to shrink the heads of their enemies after they killed them. But once he became a Christian, he stopped his tribe from fighting other tribes. He told the ministers and officers of the State, "You know, we used to smoke like you are smoking and now we believe that is wrong, it's not good for the body." And you'd see people stubbing out their cigarettes. "We used to make beer and get drunk and now we don't do that. We also used to kill those who killed us out of revenge and now we make peace, we pray for them."

So for my dad the summer of 1955 was spent in service, devotion and reflection, and when he returned, he really knew that God was saying, "It's all right, this is the right direction to go." It confirmed his sense of calling to the ministry. He recalled that when he came back and told his family and the guys around the house, they teased him:

> It was a time that the communist threat was big, and I remember thinking that I'd probably end up being captured, tortured and wouldn't live long. If communism took over the world, then certainly we would be the first ones to go. But that didn't deter me. I really felt that God was saying this is what I was called to do. At this time, I knew nothing about my mom's prayer when I was a sick baby. She didn't say anything about the prayer when I told her of this call into the ministry. My dad said, "I'm really proud of you for this decision," and then somewhere along the way he would add, "Don't you think you should go into business for a while first?"

From that time on, Dad's grades, which had suffered his first two years with all his activities, were great, even when he was elected Associated Student Body President in 1956 and worked at least 40 hours a week in that office. He had a purpose in his life and studies and knew what he was going to do to be useful.

The devotion Dad wrote, "What Makes us Great?" ends with his formula for being great. It is the purpose that Dad found that summer in Peru and spent the rest of his life pursuing.

> It seems we are always looking around to figure out who the 'great ones' are.
>
> The media fosters this question by dwelling on famous people. Some time back there was a TV show "Lifestyles of the Rich and Famous." I was as curious as you and liked to watch it to see how they lived!
>
> We can't escape hearing about Lady Gaga or Brittany Spears or Tiger Woods or Charlie Sheen. Funny thing for me is that I ask myself "who cares? And then I still read the latest scandal they've created. What is it about us?
>
> We need to be reminded that fame is a long way from greatness. Sadly, we still get confused and find ourselves wanting to be both rich and famous.
>
> Actually, the desire to be great is not such a bad ambition. There is something deep in us all that wants our lives to count for something significant! Well, if we listen to Jesus we learn what true greatness is all about: Greatness is found in serving.
>
> We have no more authentic model for greatness than in Jesus himself who "though he was in

> the form of God(!) ... emptied himself, taking the form of a slave ... and humbled himself and became obedient to the point of death, even death on a cross!" (Phil. 2:5-11)
>
> That is greatness! And the good news is that this kind of greatness is within the reach of everyone ... rich or poor, tall or short, bright or dull, old or young ... we can all serve people in need both near and far!

This devotion is so well-tuned to what I heard about my father in the days and weeks after his death. It wasn't a position or title that he held that made him a great man, but it was all the ways that he was of service to others. He approached situations, including parenting, with an intent to be useful, supportive and encouraging and the results most often matched his intent.

EIGHT

Stumble-proofing by Dick Leon, Daily Devotions,
December 2011, Volume 38, Number 12,
Northminster Presbyterian Church, Tucson, AZ

To him who is able to keep you from stumbling and to present you before his glorious presence without fault and with great joy – to the only God our Savior be glory, majesty, power and authority, through Jesus Chris our Lord, before all ages, now and forevermore! Amen. Jude 1:24-25

The New Testament has several "doxologies" in which an author wraps up a text with a word of praise and adoration to God for all his benefits to us. This doxology in Jude is one of my favorites.

God is addressed with one of our chief temptations in mind that we might stumble, or more precisely fall away from him. The allusion is to a theme that opened this little letter; false teachers who deceive us with their lies about life. It seems the main concern here was for loose living. Wow, do we ever need reminders about the problems of loose livers! We all need to stumble-proof our lives.

I THINK BACK TO HOW I FELT BY THE TIME MY BUSIness partnership ended. I was exhausted—the kind of exhaustion that comes from being in a funhouse where everything is surprising and you are constantly wary and alert because you don't know what's going to come at you next. It wasn't long before nothing about my life with my business partners was fun. I dreaded finding out what was happening. I had expected challenges associated with a quickly growing high-tech firm, challenges like miscommunication, dissatisfaction as roles and responsibilities changed, and friction caused by conflicting personalities. We certainly had those. But it was the wacky stories and dramas that really wore me down.

John [not his real name], who I liked very much even though I didn't know him well, worked on my business partner's team. We were structured so that I had my team and my business that came from the company I had owned previous to this partnership and my partner and my husband worked together on their business. I did the overall financials and introduced some of my clients to my partners so I was aware of what they were doing at a high level but not involved on a day-to-day basis. I probably would have been institutionalized long before if that had been the case.

John came to us from Microsoft around July of 2007 and was a soft-spoken, organized, capable program manager. Well-liked, he fit in immediately and wasn't a cause of any ruffle. In October, he needed to go to a friend's funeral. He went to the funeral and came back, describing the old friends that he saw there and the sadness from his friend's death of colon cancer. Nothing seemed unusual about this other than the fact that John was just in his late 20's so it was sad he had a friend of his age that had died. After our holiday party, which John and his girlfriend attended, no one saw or heard from John; yet no one thought too much of it, as the party was on Friday, December 21st, and from there through New Year's everyone scattered, taking time off or working from home.

On January 3rd, things in the office were back to "normal" except for the absence of my partners who had gone off to hang glide in Mexico. Since I was the only partner present, our HR person came to tell me that John was still not around, even after the holidays, and was not answering his phone or returning messages. We searched the Internet for his name, hoping we could find his girlfriend's number to call her. What came back, the absolutely first entry, was a memo from the Department of Justice, dated October 26, 2007, the same day as his friend's "funeral":

> "John ..., 27, of ...., Wash., was sentenced today by U.S. District Judge ...... for his involvement in an Internet software piracy ring, Assistant Attorney General ..... announced.
>
> ".... was sentenced to 12 months in prison on a felony count of conspiracy to infringe copyright."

The memo laid out the timeline. John had been indicted in 2006, about a year before he came to work with us, was sentenced in October, and then had two months post sentencing before having to report to a minimum security prison.

My business partner always seemed involved somehow in odd happenings. One time, aware that there was a bench warrant out for his arrest because of unpaid traffic tickets, he traded cars with one of our clients, an attorney and a friend of mine from before I'd even met either my husband or my partner. Rather than take care of his situation, my partner asked our client to switch cars with him. He figured no cop would be looking for him in the client's car. I called my friend, the client, and asked, "What are you thinking?" He thought the whole thing was hilarious! He wanted my partner working on his project instead of taking care of little details like bench warrants. I was relieved that he was unconcerned but also flabbergasted. After all, he was an attorney! Was I the crazy one here?

In one of the last odd incidents, which came shortly before everything fell apart completely, my partner hired the father of a former employee who had left only six weeks earlier in a very unhappy state. I'm not sure of the exact circumstances of the departure, but in my office on the 2nd floor of an 80-year-old office building, I felt the reverberations of a lot of door slamming underneath me. Later, when I followed up with her on making the company's 401k matching payment, she was quick to say, "You can take the money and stuff it." I never worked out a full explanation of how all of this came to pass but several things were clear: My partner knew the employee had left angrily, he hired the new employee and he knew he was her father. The father, not a replacement for the work she had done, lived in California and had a job description that was generic enough that there was a plentiful pool of candidates in the Seattle area. Definitely, my partner had a higher tolerance for messiness than I did.

In our company, there was a lot of talent and energy and a wider interpretation of rules and boundaries than I had grown up with. My husband and I had ongoing debates like this: "Is it okay to park in the Baskin and Robbins parking lot when it is closed so that you can go in to the Starbucks next door to get a coffee to go?" My answer, unequivocally no, open or closed, because it is their property, and they've put up no parking signs and there are other places to park even if it takes a couple more minutes to find them and walk. My husband's answer was unequivocally yes. His thinking was that Baskin and Robbins wasn't using the space at the time so what's the big deal? My partner's answer? I don't think that we ever had that debate, but I imagine that it would be something like it was fine for him to park his car inside the Starbucks if he could charm the barista enough to let him do it.

When I started to meditate, I got some relief from my exhaustion. The danger was now over and I could start to breathe. My spirit, that reservoir of energy, belief and joy, felt just a little bit lighter each time, as if it was being unstuck one breath at a time. My perspective widened from my situation as I did something positive and proactive. I was reminded of the Native American story of a grandfather who describes two men to his grandson, one selfish and warring and the other caring and generous. When his grandson asks which one he will grow up to be, the grandfather replies, "It depends on which one you feed." I was finally mindful of what I was feeding.

Reflecting on my dad's devotion, Stumble-proofing, I can identify with stumbling, with living with loose boundaries and then trying to cope with the aftermath. It ate up so much positive momentum that I was used to having in my life. I was far more appreciative of the boundary-filled existence of my childhood and ready to be much more careful about choosing a path going forward.

Dad finishes "Stumble-proofing" with these observations:
> We live in a culture that erases the moral boundaries that once held us all accountable. These days it is not just a matter of "anything goes." It is more a matter of "everything wild and crazy is encouraged" in order to live the good life!

I love the quote that comes from Dostoyevsky's classic novel, *Brothers Karamazov*. Carolyn and I have had a friend print it in calligraphy and we have posted it on our wall. It goes like this:

"When transcendence disappears, everything is permissible."

As soon as we cut God out of the picture, we lose our bearings; we have no fixed points of reference, no firm boundaries, and no reliable fences around our desires.

So, Jude reminds us that there is One who can keep us from stumbling and from falling on our face in the mud, and that One is our only God, our Savior, whom we know through Jesus Christ, our Lord. He is forever true and forever present and forever on our side. He is our Transcendent One who keeps our lives in order and in balance! Hang on tightly to him, he will keep you from stumbling!

So much of Dad's writing came from his personal experience, but I can't find much stumbling or ever falling away from the discipline of his beliefs in his life story. He did, however, spend two years living in India and I wonder if the experience of living in such a different culture with unfamiliar rules and boundaries confirmed the conviction of his beliefs.

Dad had started at Princeton Theological Seminary in the fall of 1957 to pursue his Masters of Divinity. Princeton Theological Seminary, founded in 1812, was the first seminary affiliated with the Presbyterian Church and also the largest. Most of the Presbyterian pastors he knew had graduated from there and he had chosen it because it was the most prestigious, demanding and balanced theological seminary. It had conservative and liberal wings, and Dad thought it would be good getting out of the West to experience the challenge of East Coast Ivy League culture. He said, "I wanted to get the best education I could and Princeton had that reputation." His coursework included Biblical studies, theology, church history, homiletics (preaching), and practical theology.

NINE

***The Good, the Right and the True** by Dick Leon,
Daily Devotions, January, 2009, Volume 36, Number 1,
Northminster Presbyterian Church, Tucson, AZ*

*For you were once darkness, but now you are light in the Lord.
Live as children of light (for the fruit of the light consists in all
goodness, righteousness and truth).
Ephesians 5:8-9*

Darkness is dangerous.

AFTER DAD'S SECOND YEAR OF THE THREE-YEAR SEMInary program at Princeton, a couple of pastors, Ren Jackson and Bill Cohea, founders of the International Studies Program (ISP), came to the Princeton campus to talk with students about studying abroad. The rationale of their program was that Western culture had made a huge impact on Eastern culture through colonialism, commercialism, capitalism, democracy, and technology. But at the time, the late 1950's, the East and Eastern religions were beginning to make an impact on the West, and it could be seen in Buddhist art forms and in disciplines like yoga. The goal of ISP was to accomplish two things: one, to immerse future pastors in Eastern philosophies, religions and cultures so that they would be able to understand better how to relate with them, and secondly, to inaugurate an experimental form of mission. Traditional mission had been more or less an approach of "I'm coming to your country as a missionary to tell you the truth." Bill and Ren wanted future pastors to embody incarnational ministry, to go live with people and relate from the inside, just as God came in Christ, dwelling among us and becoming one with us. The idea was to replicate that pattern, to go as a student, study the history and culture and understand the people. So after two years in his graduate program at Princeton, Dad decided to really get out of the West and study abroad in India. He reported, "Again there was a deep sense inside that God was saying, 'This is what I want you to do. You need to go to India!'"

Dad raised $2,400 to cover expenses for the next two years, in part from churches and individuals that sponsored his mission. It was a tight budget that he spent carefully and he felt accountable to those supporters, writing many letters with carbon copies to report on his experiences. The budget was six hundred dollars to get to India, the same for the return and $50 a month to cover room, board, tuition, travel around the county, supplies like bedding and clothing, and a bike. He describes the final leg of the trip to arrive in India in a letter to one supporter: "By the time we passed through Afghanistan, first by plane and then the last two days on the top of a tumbly truck bouncing our way across the desert and in to the mountain passes and then through Pakistan by train, foot and bus, in the midst of a new degree of heat and dirt, we were really ready to arrive in India and be able to call it our home."

In his recollections, the idea of going to India and his ensuing experience taught him two things: 1) the incarnational approach worked, he said, "Students who later became good friends told me that had they known initially that I was training to become a Christian pastor, they never would have engaged me in conversation and eventual friendship." And 2) he saw who he was when there were huge challenges when "all of the normal, emotional supports for survival were gone ... things like cleanliness, orderliness, available resources, everything was different."

Before Dad left to study in India, his parents flew out to Princeton to see him off. During that visit, when Dad was 24 years old, his mom finally revealed her secret to him. Dad recalled what she told him:

> I was so sick as a baby at Providence Hospital and afterwards for nearly two years that Mom at some point prayed for God to spare me and she would dedicate me to God for whatever He wanted to do with my life. She could not tell the story without crying, but that was not exactly unusual because I think every time I left home she cried. It was a very touching time and became a confirmation that the decision I'd made, first of all, to become a Christian, and then four years after that to enter into ministry, and now four years later to go to India all seemed to be doing just what the Lord had intended for me. The sequence of Mom's prayer and my ministry decisions all through my life have often come to mind and have always had the same effect of telling me that my life has been in God's hands from the start.

The study program that Dad pursued starting the fall of 1959 was in Ancient Indian History, Culture and Archeology, also called Indology. He earned an MA degree from Benares Hindu University, the premier of four national Hindu universities in India because it was located on the Ganges River in the ancient center of Hinduism and Buddhism, Benares (also called Varanasi).

Once arriving in India, Dad started to learn Hindi from a fellow in the untouchable class, Sham Narayan, who earned money to go to school there by being a language tutor. He lived in a neighboring village just across a small gully from the campus. The environment that Dad found himself in was wrenching.

> Although the university was located out a ways from the city, Benares itself, one of the oldest cities in the world with its narrow gullies and winding streets, was another world altogether. There is no way to describe the adjustments needed to deal with the heat, the language, the meaning of time, the animals, the food, the patterns of conversation and the smells. The University campus had an openness and uniformity of architecture that was very orderly, with university buildings at the core and then athletic buildings, sport fields and dormitories built on a circular pattern around them. All this made life on the campus much easier to live in, but it still was terribly foreign and thoroughly Indian, a long way from home.

He may have been living in a culture with a different sense of time, but Dad was still moving at his same speed and was quickly elected president of the International House. Except for Jim Bakeman, his partner in the program, whom he knew not only from Princeton but also from the University of Washington, there were no other Americans there among the Asian foreigners, Buddhists monks and Germans. Fortunately, the food they served the students was a little less spicy than the average Indian fare. Even after he and Jim moved into a student hostel, they continued to eat at the International House. Later when they chose a mess hall with purely Indian food, they faced another huge adjustment, being sick the first six months with Delhi belly or Benares bowels, whatever you want to call it. The first time they ate in the mess hall everyone gathered around to watch. After being served a curry, Dad had taken no more than two bites before he had sweat pouring from under his eyelids, upper lip, forehead, armpits, everywhere. Of course, his reaction to the heat was to gulp down water and try to douse the fire. But the water wasn't boiled as it had been at the International House, so it just compounded the problem several fold. Finally, about six months later, Jim and he had so many antibodies running through them, Dad felt that he could take almost anything. His letters mention the food repeatedly but also the social life:

> Our hostel is a single row of 20'x30' rooms in the shape of a square with an open garden in the center. The latrine (their words, not ours) is kitty-corner from mine and it necessitates passing one or two sides of the square to get there. This leaves one open to many opportunities to be called, commanded or invited into a room with anywhere from one to five students to discuss subjects ranging from law, to engineering, to America, women, and research on 'destiny and fate.' One fellow just left my room after 45 minutes of discussing Napoleon, Hindu soul and what is good and what is evil.

A couple months into the second academic year, Dad contracted Hepatitis A and rested and recuperated while staying with the Harlands, who were English missionaries, for about six weeks. They lived halfway between the campus and downtown Benares on one of the main roads. Wonderful hosts and nurses, they provided Dad with Western food and a comfortable bed, instead of his board bed with a mattress of two sheets pressed together.

Dad weathered these wrenching adjustments and serious illness because of his belief that he was supposed to be there. He writes in a letter,

> Please try not to yourself or let others in their minds think of us as great missionaries or pioneers or adventurers or any such thing. We are not really living a life any more difficult than any of you in God's plan and in some way ours is easier because it is not the ordinary. As BP [Blaise Pascal] says, "The strength of a man's virtue must not be measured by his efforts but by his ordinary life." So with all of us. I cringe at some thoughts written to us that we are 'heroic.' We only seek to let God continue to mold us in this environment whereas you do the same in yours and to try and permit his message to continue to communicate through us as it has come to us through others. Our lives are different in form, expression, location but not in quality!

He described his sense of faith during this time in India as a strong conviction of God's protection that might seem a bit naive to others because he could have died. In fact, another Princeton student who came on the same program during Dad's second year also contracted hepatitis and did die of it after less than one year in India. Dad recalled, "My feeling of safety came from the belief that God called me here and I'm going to be fine. I was just doing what I thought God called me to do – it was a simple act of obedience for me. That conviction made all the difference in the world on making it through the challenges of those two years."

Jim Harland was the pastor of the Anglican church, which was on the other side of Benares in the cantonment, a section of town where the British had their military base. This was the church that Dad attended although they only held a service there every two weeks. He would bike all the way across town, which could take up to an hour, to join about 25 people who showed up for worship. In the second year, 1961, Queen Elizabeth II of England and Prince Phillip visited Benares and the little Anglican church. Dad's recollection was, "They got a new rug for the center aisle, a royal blue one with a gold fleur de lis in it. The place otherwise looked shabby. And those of us who were regulars got seats up front and, of course, the place was packed. I was just six feet from the Queen and Prince Phillip as they walked through the gathered throng after the service."

When Dad took Mom on her first visit to India in 1974, she was able to see the Anglican Church. She recalled:

> We had been at the Taj Mahal the day before in 118 degree heat. Even though we had come from the Philippines and were used to the heat, in India the heat was so intense that we both drank loads of water in our lovely hotel. They assured us it was boiled but it obviously wasn't and we became very sick. The little Anglican Church was right across the courtyard from our hotel, and I wanted to go

> see it because I'd heard so many royal stories. I managed to drag myself out of bed and without your father crept across the street and sought refuge in the church. There was a plaque on the wall, not saying Richard Leon had been here, but that the Queen and Prince Phillip had been here.

In the summer of 1960, during the university break, Dad and Jim Bakeman, his partner in the program, decided to explore separately. Tension existed between them, seemingly because Dad was adjusting to India better than Jim. Jim was left-handed which was a terrible disadvantage because you eat with your hands and left hands were associated with private hygiene, so he had to change to his right hand. Dad was more social, likely more social than everyone, and more athletic, while Jim was more academic and introverted in a country that was very verbal. They separated to travel but planned to meet later in a Christian ashram in Kerala, a state in Southern India.

Dad traveled through India, to Calcutta, up to Darjeeling, where he met Tenzing Norgay just seven years after his first successful summit of Mt. Everest, then down to Madras, visiting the homes of friends from the university, and then finally to Kerala.

If his limited budget chafed at the time, there is no sign of it in his recollection as he delightedly told me of the details.

> I traveled 5,000 miles and I think it cost $200 or something like that because I had a student pass and went third class. In third class, the people would ask, "Where are you from?" and I'd always answer, "Guess, you tell me." Invariably the first guess would be Germany or Russia. And then England and then maybe Australia. One guy

guessed Japan, I don't know why. But when I told them America, they'd say, "No, you're not from America. No American travels third class and dresses like an Indian and has his whole life rolled into a bister."

We used a bister [translates to bed in Urdu] to carry all our stuff. It's a big canvas case with a small flap on each end to hold your one-inch thick mattress and all your clothing. When you roll it up, it's your whole luggage and your bed roll. The best way to travel is to get a train boy to take you back to where the train originates before it comes into the station so you can get a position on the luggage rack before the train fills up. I would get up there and think I was in good shape but before the train got more than five miles out of the station, there would be five of us sitting up there.

To visit a student friend and his family in a village was India at its purest. People were simple, they were hospitable, they lived together with mixed religions, the whole setting was very harmonious. But after a visit in a village halfway between Calcutta and Madras, I had to get back on a train when it was already full. So, sitting on a platform that is packed full, I watch the train coming into the station. The whole platform rises up like a horde of angry insects and rushes the train. I had three or four trains go by before I figured out what to do. Finally, I decided to go for it. I threw my bister in a window, jumped onto the entry steps and grabbed on. It was already full but I grabbed on anyway. There were two steps outside the train, I had one guy behind me, and we took off. On the little entryway in front of us about 3 feet by 6 feet I counted 25 people. Off the entryway was the toilet that was a hole in the floor and three people were in there! Until somebody needed it and then they would have to come join the 25 of us. We traveled like this for about an hour, until enough people got off and I could get into the entryway. And it was another hour before I could finally get inside to find my bister somewhere in the carriage. That was about the craziest travel experience I had, but I wasn't alone, everybody else was doing it.

Arriving at the Christian ashram, Dad found a serious state of affairs. Jim had arrived at the ashram and then had gone for a walk through town out to a little waterway. Because Americans were so noticeable, kids had been watching him and recognized rat poison because they used it often for its intended purpose. They watched him spread the poison on a piece of bread and told their elders who were able to get Jim to a hospital. He had taken a bunch of aspirin in preparation for eating the sandwich but they pumped his stomach before much damage had been done. Unfortunately, he was under police arrest for breaking a law in the suicide attempt, and the American consulate needed to get involved to get him released.

Jim was not very verbal through his hospitalization and release, but he and Dad went back to the ashram, which means resting place, for a brief respite before Jim left for Delhi. They put

Dad and Jim in one room with two beds, each on opposite walls and one light bulb, hanging in the middle of the room. After they went to bed that first night, a huge storm came through and lightning struck their room, racing down the light bulb and through to the switch on the wall, blowing the power to the entire building, followed immediately by a huge thunder clap. It was 3 AM. Dad hadn't been sleeping because he was worried about Jim, and was sitting up on his bed with his back to the wall, praying and thinking. So he saw the whole thing transpire. Jim, however, had been in a deep sleep and was totally unnerved, screaming and panicking. When they finally got some candles and had restored some sense of calm, Dad decided to move his bed next to Jim's so that Jim would have to climb over Dad if he were to leave the room.

Dad related what happened next as they lay there in the dark:

> I'm lying there with my arm stretched out and then Jim reaches over and grabs my arm at the elbow and I grab his. Jim's grasp has the feel of a death-grip to it. Then, the strangest thing happens as we are lying there connected this way. It's almost as if whatever dark spirits are in him, the ones that drove him to suicide, are now in me. I feel depressed, something like suicidal, dark and self-destructive, as if his spirit and mine are mingled. I remembered in seminary we had studied the Desert Fathers who often felt as if they wrestled with the devil. They would offer a simple prayer, 'In the name of Jesus, be gone,' believing His is the last name the devil can stand. I'm thinking I need to pray this command but then I find I couldn't say a thing, I couldn't get words out."

> In my mind, I say two or three times, 'In the name of Jesus, be gone.' After the second or third time, Jim's hand goes totally limp and I let go of him as well. He stirs a little bit and I ask if he's okay. He says in the first calm voice I had heard from him since his suicide attempt, 'Yeah,' and we go to sleep.

Dad was still astonished 53 years later as he told the story, the raw power of the moment evident in his face, his eyes pensive and without their usual shine. He said by the next day Jim's spirit was totally different as if this dark spirit or mood had been exorcised and his healing had really begun.

Dad didn't tell that part of the India story very often. In his letters, there is barely a mention of Jim's leaving as he didn't feel it would be right to stigmatize him in any way. But I find in a letter dated December 22, 1959, six months before the suicide attempt, an explanation of two different men, Dad, who was sure he was on the right path and able to survive all the sickness and adjustment because of it. And Jim, who was suffering, perhaps because he was on a path that wasn't quite right for him and he was unsure of how to move off of it:

> [Jim] feels totally inadequate for what we are doing here and would readily like to escape to an ashram or some such retreat. My reply was only that perhaps this is where we should always be, in despair to ourselves and finally in reliance upon Him who only can make this time fruitful.
>
> Another source of Jim's frustration has been an insecurity for being here. This I think has stemmed though from the feeling of failure, but may I emphasize that such failure will only stand

the world's test of superficialisms, for actually I feel he has done much; with those about him and within himself. But his questions have brought me to do the same and to find that some of my security here is from the feeling of purposefulness and proper placement.

While I've found some sermons from very early on in Dad's career where he references meditation as sitting to gaze at one's navel in contrast to Christianity where the view is outward towards God, I know that Dad was very aware of and had made an effort to study the different experiences of the Divine.

Fifty years after Dad returned from studying in India, our conversations about meditation and Eastern philosophy would certainly prove to be bolstered by understandings that he developed during his incarnational ministry, which taught him to forge relationships with, rather than convert, those whose culture and beliefs greatly differed from his.

Dad finished "The Good, The Right and the True" devotion with what he learned that night with Jim:

> Have you noticed that when we read crime stories in the paper they are almost always about incidents that happened late at night, in the dark? Darkness carries the illusion to us of secrecy and helps us think we can do nasty things and not be seen.
>
> Paul uses this imagery of being in the dark to describe what life was like for us before we came to know Jesus Christ as Lord and Savior. And then he gives three great marks of what it is to live in the light of Jesus Christ:

- **What is Good** ... the quality of doing kind and thoughtful things that build up others, family, friends and even strangers.
- **What is Right** ... the quality of having the wisdom and courage to serve the cause of justice in our world.
- **What is True** ... the quality of speaking the truth at all times and always being true to our word.

These three qualities find their polar opposites in the dark: what is Bad ... Wrong ... and False. What happens in the dark destroys and hurts and tears down. What happens in the light heals and helps and builds up.

Paul gives us a wonderfully simple three-way test for what it means to walk in the light as a follower of Jesus Christ: is it good ... right ... and true? When we do this we will indeed be followers of him who said he was the Way, the Truth and the Life ... for he is the only one in all history who always was Good, always was Right and always was True!

Dad described two distinct paths in this devotion. I haven't seen life that clearly, but as I meditated and talked with Dad about his life, I was able to see the path I had chosen with much greater clarity. Because I hadn't stumble-proofed my life, I had gotten in over my head in creating relationships in marriage and business that didn't support the best person that I could be. Any small fixes that I tried to apply once I was in that position were completely ineffective. Dad's confidence in the Good, the Right and the True is infectious; it inspires me to find my way to the right path.

TEN

***Healing, If We Want It** by Dick Leon, Daily Devotions, January 2013, Volume 40, Number 1, Northminster Presbyterian Church, Tucson, AZ*

When Jesus saw him lying there and learned that he had been in this condition for a long time, he asked him, "Do you want to get well?" John 5:6

I HAVE A FRIEND, 10 YEARS OLDER, WHO WAS GOING through a bitterly fought second divorce around the same time that I was going through my own divorce. By the time it was done all the houses he had owned and savings he had accumulated were gone. He had been married twice as long, 16 years to my 8, and had kids. My divorce was not contentious, and there was nothing like contrast to make me grateful that my situation wasn't worse. "Do you mean at age 50, I have to start all over?" he asked. I was finding out that you can be done with a marriage, physically and legally, without being finished with the chapter.

Living in Seattle, there are many places where you round a corner and are faced suddenly with a view of Mt. Rainier. It is "the mountain" and when it appears, it is achingly beautiful. One morning in my late twenties, I was crawling along southbound I-5 to where it fed to eastbound I-90 in early morning rush hour traffic, and Mt. Rainier jumped into my view in a way that took my breath away. I thought, "I want to climb that mountain." I discovered in that effort what I now recognize as my first meditation practice.

The first attempt was on a standard guided climb with twenty-four total climbers, two of whom were my good friends, Jeff and Doug. Doug has done everything out-doorsy at least once and seems to do it all well. He has a fantastic story of his first experience climbing Mt. Hood as a 16 year old with his grandfather. At some point high up on the mountain, his grandfather couldn't go on, so he asked a team of young 20-something climbers to take his grandson up to the top on their rope. They summited, returned Doug to his grandfather and said Doug could climb with them anytime. The leader wrote his number, "Jon Krakauer, 503-555-1212."

On the first day of that climb of Rainier we made it to the hut at Camp Muir at 10,000 feet carrying full packs. As we staked out our bunks, the lead guide came in and started quoting Robert Service poetry:

There is a race of men who won't fit in,
A race that can't stand still.
So they break the hearts of kith and kin,
And roam the world at will.

It stormed that evening after dinner. We watched as the clouds rolled in. From on top of the clouds we experienced lightning unleashed beneath us. A breathtaking view, I felt that I was on Mt. Olympus witnessing Zeus hurl lightning bolts on the world. Packed in the bunkhouse on cramped wooden ledges, we tried to sleep or rest as we waited for our chance to climb. The guides woke us every hour to tell us it was still storming. Finally at 6 am, they said we could try it, except that we were 6 hours behind schedule so anyone attempting to climb would have to climb twice as fast. We left with a pared down team because half of the group thought twice as fast sounded crazy. Doug, Jeff and I made it to the next rest break at 11,500 ft before calling it quits; the pace was brutal, especially in the fresh snow. But the images of that trip, the poetry, the packs, the storm, the camaraderie, the awe of what was left to climb burned deeply into me. When I climb, the repetition numbs my mind and the focus is all about the breath—the ultimate walking meditation.

I summited on my next attempt, a five-day guided expedition on the mountain where we learned to set up rescue pulleys, ice-climbed in crevasses and summited. The meal the first night was tostadas, the guides actually managing to get the chips up to 9,000 ft without breaking them into unmanageable pieces. The food on a trip is both awful and amazing simultaneously but gratitude seems so easy to find on a mountain.

I've climbed most with my friend, Jill, who is a far more accomplished climber than I. We started climbing separately, each summiting Rainier before we were really close but then forged a deeper relationship traipsing around together. Jill and I have climbed in the Pacific NW—Mt. Adams, Mt. Baker (she and Doug summited, I did not), Mt. St. Helens, and Rainier. We also climbed in Mexico, where we met our friend, Sue, married to one of the best climbers and guides of all time, Phil Ershler. On that trip we climbed Ixtaccihuatl and attempted Orizaba before we turned back because of conditions. I hiked in the 38 miles to Everest Base Camp with Sue and Phil before one of their Everest attempts. We've trekked the

Inca trail to Macchu Pichu, joined by our friend, Kellie, on a trip that Phil and Sue planned, and climbed Via Ferrata routes in the Dolomites on a trip that Jill put together. Climbing has built a deep sense of community and connection for me with these friends, Jill, Sue, Kellie, Doug and their families, especially Christine, Indigo, Aiden and Dana, that have seen us off, picked us up, allowed us the time to be in the mountains and listened endlessly to the reminiscences. The connection resonates with each story that we remember, the stories told about the trip and also the stories that are told when we are waiting around for water to boil or night to fall. The memories forged in thinner air seem to be more solid. "Do you remember the time we did the narcolepsy tour of Rainier?" we'll say. This was an attempt where we never even made it past 10,000 feet and we had a good idea when we left the parking lot at 5,400 feet that we wouldn't be able to climb because of avalanche danger. We doddled, taking breaks every 200 feet or so it seemed. Jill, Doug and I still talk about that trip even though nothing happened except Doug fell asleep during a break on Moon Rocks and woke himself up snoring.

Getting to the top of a mountain feels like a Divine test. It's often windy and cold and the chill sets in immediately once I've stopped moving, the air is thin and I'm exhausted. The moment is huge and the view is well-earned, even if it is 360 degrees of a cloud layer beneath us with just other mountain tops poking through as it often is in the Pacific Northwest. It's a physical realization of the spiritual – everything is momentous, the view, the accomplishment, the exhilaration and yet I can't stay there because I'm tiny. I see the manifestation of my place in the universe, I'm small, my concerns are small and this life is huge, far more than I can see or understand.

Now my divorcing friend and I were travelling along winding state road 504 East to Mt. Saint Helens to meet Jill and attempt to climb it in the winter. It was just a few weeks shy of the 30th anniversary of the 1980 eruption and the Park Service lets all registered climbers attempt the climb during the winter season when the slopes are protected by snow. Permits for the mountain are limited in the summer season so that the vegetation has less foot traffic as it tries to rebound. In the 1980 eruption, the mountain lost 1,312 feet off the top, replacing the summit dome with a large crater. Only 8,365 feet high, it's a long one-day hike to the crater rim and back with about 1,000 feet more vertical climbing in the winter because you start from a lower parking lot. We would figure out that the mountain was showing us the way, that renewal is a way of life.

The wind was blowing sideways at 30mph and the route was completely iced over. We had planned and worked out for months in preparation, but we readily accepted that summiting St. Helens on this divorce conversation trip wasn't going to happen. It was so easy to release that ambition because my spiritual perspective was balanced when climbing: the mountain is big and I am small. I came to see that closing out the chapter on my marriage was akin to turning back on a climb. I had to have faith that life is bigger than I can see. I had to give up my struggle to find emotional traction on the path I was on in order to take up a new route.

A passage from *Book of Awakening* sums it up:

> I know now that, over the years, my own cries that life is unfair have come from the inescapable pain of living, and these cries, while understandable, have always diverted me from feeling my way through the pain of my breakage into the reformation of my life. Somehow, crying "Unfair" has always kept me stuck in what hurts.

Pema Chödrön in her book, *Living Beautifully with Uncertainty and Change*, calls this particular spiritual crisis ego "clinging"—the idea that we have a fixed identity that gives us a sense of false security. We then fight experiences that threaten our identity. She continues to describe using a spiritual path and meditation to erode that fixed identity:

> The purpose of the spiritual path is to unmask, to take off our armor. When that happens, it feels like a crisis because it *is* a crisis – a fixed identity crisis. The Buddha taught that the fixed identity is the cause of our suffering. Looking deeper, we could say that the real cause of suffering is not being able to tolerate uncertainty – and thinking that it's perfectly sane, perfectly normal, to deny the fundamental groundlessness of being human.

There is a lot of potential for ego clinging in the life of a pastor, especially when he retires. Dad believed quite adamantly that when a pastor retires or leaves a church for any reason, he must break from the church he led in order to give the new pastor a chance to build his or her own relationships within that community. That meant, in the case where the pastor stays in the area as Mom and Dad did, he must say "no" to performing weddings and funerals for people from that church and for a time turn down all speaking engagements, and find a new place to worship. An ego-clinging challenge of the highest order. Dad wrote about this philosophy in an article "Never Can Say Goodbye" in the November 2006 issue of *Presbyterians Today*:

> Pastors can be proactive in setting the stage for their successors. This applies to all pastors, as-

sociate pastors, and long-term staff leaders. All those active in ministry have "loyalists." Leaders can give people permission to love those who will succeed them and teach that such love is in no way a betrayal or competition with the love they share. Even more important, pastors can challenge their friends to remain active and strong in support of those who follow.

Pastors need to get their egos out of the way and to demonstrate the highest ethical standards. They are called to model the spiritual maturity of "dying to self" in order to make an honorable separation from congregations.

During Dad's funeral, Dr. Scott Dudley told the story of what happened when Dad retired from Bellevue Presbyterian Church and Scott was chosen to succeed him. He said that Dad refused all pastoral services, even when Scott begged him. But they would meet for breakfast and Scott would relay the challenges on his plate. Dad's response followed a pattern. First, he would nod his head and say, "Hmm, that is hard." Then, he'd follow up with a little theology and some very practical advice. Finally, Dad would say, "You can do it. You are doing great."

But then Scott made a decision that he knew Dad wouldn't have agreed with or made. The next time they had breakfast, he told Dad about the decision and let him know that if anyone asked, Dad was free to say he disagreed. Dad said, "Hmm, that is hard." Then he said, "If anyone asks, you just tell them that Dick Leon is 100% with you on this."

Dad knew the secret to being not only done but also finished. Just let go. Trust that you are in Divine hands that will help you to be honorable and find a new path. In his devotion, "Healing, If We Want it," he wrote:

> I can still remember when I was in grade school and I had something happening at school that I didn't want to experience, (Maybe a test? Or a game I wasn't good at?) I would feign illness! I didn't always get away with this, but it worked well enough for me to get pretty good at being 'sick.'
>
> If my Mom were to ask me at that time, "Do you want to get well?" I probably would have told her, "No, it is really quite useful for me to be sick right now!" Of course, that level of honest conversation never happened.
>
> Illness can be useful to us. I find it to be a great excuse for bad golf days. It is also a way people can evade intimacy in a relationship, or escape from an unwelcome invitation to a party, and even a way of avoiding responsibility.
>
> So, when Jesus asks this seemingly silly question to the paralytic, we must know that it isn't so silly after all. The man may have worked up a pretty good strategy for living paralyzed and if he were well, he would have to buck up and be a producer and provider for himself. It turns out he did want to get well, and Jesus delivered!
>
> There is a wonderful saying, carved on the mantel of a half-way house where young people live after spending time in jail for breaking the law. It goes like this: "DO YOU WANT TO BE RIGHT ... OR WELL?"

Jesus offers us wholeness and wellness. But we have to want it and all the joys, obligations and responsibilities that come with being fit.

Part of my emotional struggle with accepting defeat in my marriage came from wanting the solidity that Mom and Dad had created in their marriage. They made a lifelong partnership seem so natural. I hadn't done that yet, but setting out on climbing adventures in conditions that were not right for summiting allowed me to understand that defeat can mean I had survived to climb again. I have hope that my ability to create a partnership will follow and add to the many other parallels between our lives: I hiked to Everest base camp a little more than fifty years after Dad was in India and met Tenzing Norgay, the first Sherpa to summit Mt. Everest, fifty-five years after Dad visited Machu Picchu following his summer mission work in Peru, I trekked the Inca trail to see it, and fifty years after Mom graduated from college with her degree in Far Eastern studies, I followed in the footsteps of her love of Russia (a country she visited many times over the years) by attempting Mt. Elbrus in the Caucasus Mountains.

ELEVEN

The Lord's Internal Exam by Dick Leon, Daily Devotions, March 2012, Volume 39, Number 3, Northminster Presbyterian Church, Tucson, AZ

His pleasure is not in the strength of the horse, nor his delight in the legs of the warrior; the LORD delights in those who fear him, who put their hope in his unfailing love. Ps. 14:10-11

WORKING WITH MY DAD ON ANY PROJECT WAS THE polar opposite of meditation. He was so fast-moving that by the end of the day, my nervous system would be completely wrung out from trying to keep up with him. When it came to doing things, he had a sense of urgency that was hard to match, and I don't typically doddle. This applied to playing tennis, working on a project, and even walking. I swear that at times even Biscuit couldn't keep up with Dad, and Biscuit is no slouch either. Dad was pretty amazing as a role model, consistent between his words and actions, but when he would tell me to go slow on something, ha!

I imagine that coming back from India had something to do with the speed with which he wooed my mom. In his stories of India he alluded to a different sense of time in that culture. It must have driven him nuts. Returning, still within his $600 budget, he literally took the slow boat that left from Bombay, stopped in Colombo (Ceylon), Singapore, Saigon, Hong Kong and finally docked in Yokohama. He flew home from there. How he must have been itching to go!

Dad was 26 years old and spent the summer in Seattle before returning to Princeton to finish his last year of seminary. Both Mom and Dad had heard of each other from mutual friends who insisted they should meet. My mother was a beautiful, smart and independent 22 year old. As I search the *Seattle Times* archives for both of my parents, it is my mom who shows up in more articles than my dad. While she was at the University of Washington, she was a Phi Beta Kappa and active in Mortar Board events as well as church activities and sorority events in the Kappa Kappa Gamma house. She graduated from the University of Washington with a BA in Far Eastern studies, was recruited by the CIA and passed all the qualification tests, but she tells us she didn't want to be holed up all day in an office translating Russian documents. "Can you imagine a better cover than being a pastor's wife?" is a family joke.

It was Earl Palmer, college pastor at UPC following Gary Demarest, who suggested my dad meet Carolyn Vandiver. Even though Dad had heard of Mom from several people, she proved to be elusive in May of 1961. Dad spoke at Calvin Club, the college group of about 300 students at University Presbyterian but she wasn't there although Earl said, "She never misses." And then Dad spoke at an annual deputation meeting and even though my mother had gone on deputation to New Mexico, she wasn't at the deputation meeting either.

My mom had also heard a lot about Dick Leon and knows of at least one opportunity to meet him that she intentionally passed up. She recalled, "I remember walking across campus one day and running into a friend from Calvin Club. He said he was going to have coffee with Dick Leon, and I responded, 'Oh, yeah, I've heard about him, but still haven't met him. What does he look like?' He answered, 'Well, he's not real tall and has sort of a red, round face.'" This is patently unfair, Dad was 5'10" with beautiful skin that tanned to a warm brown and set off his twinkly brown eyes, but he hadn't taken off the weight yet that he put on in India from drinking buffalo's milk – about 25 pounds. Mom answered, 'Well, I think I'll go to the library to study.'"

Dick and Carolyn finally met on the evening of my mom's 22nd birthday, June 13th. Dad seemed to have a perfect recollection of how it happened:

> I had one more year in seminary, and in the Presbyterian church before your last year you have to give a progress report to Presbytery, which consists of the pastors and elders of the churches in the area. So, I made my little presentation and was going out into the parking lot when a very lovely, young lady comes up to me, extends her hand and says, "Hi, I'm Carolyn Vandiver." I actually said to myself, "So this is the one, huh!"

But Dad couldn't get a date until July because every time he'd ask, she'd say, "Oh, I can't, I'm tied up." Dad was working at an autoclave, lifting cement blocks and trying to lose weight to get in shape. He'd start at six in the morning and be through by 2 pm or 3 pm, and then would go back to the church where she worked and chat with her. He was speaking at various church groups on his Indian experiences, including at a weekend retreat where Mom was present.

In July they finally went out. Dad described taking her to Snoqualmie Falls Lodge and thinking, "This is a classy place, so she had better be impressed! After all, I am four years older, I've had two years of seminary, I've been around the world, I was student body president, and I'm going to take her to the nicest place in the Northwest." Dad didn't finish his chicken because he was trying to lose weight and Mom was starving. After graduation, she had started rooming with a Russian family because she wanted to improve her limited Russian conversational skills. But she had not yet worked out all the nuances of sharing a kitchen and so was going hungry much of the time.

"Are you going to finish your dinner?" my mom asked.

"I think I've had enough."

So Mom consumed the remnants and Dad remembered thinking, "This is kind of cheeky for a first date!" But he liked what he saw. She wasn't nervous in the least. She was comfortable being herself. "I don't know what she's thinking but *I'm* impressed!"

By the first weekend in August, fast-moving Dad was ready to ask Mom to marry him. It was Seafair weekend, and they were viewing the action at friends of Dad's family, right above Mount Baker Park directly over the hydroplane pits. After watching the first race of three heats, Dad suggested watching the next race at his parents' house to avoid traffic later on. It was his ploy to get away from the crowd and, knowing his parents were at the race, he would be alone with her. When they got there, he gave it a gamble and declared, "I love you very much and would like to spend the rest of my life with you. Will you marry me?" And she answered . . . "Yes!"

When we were young, my mom would say this short courtship was fine because they "were older and knew what they wanted."

As we kids neared the ages of their engagement, the line became, "Don't you ever do that!"

Thinking it was honorable to ask her father's permission even though they had never met, Dad phoned her father, Dick Vandiver, in Yakima and explained, "This is Dick Leon and I've just asked your daughter to marry me. I would like to ask your permission." Dick V. commented, "Let's see, now you're the guy from India, right?" Fortunately, Mom had mentioned Dad in at least one of her letters home that summer. Then her father continued, "Well, you know what, she's of age, and she can make up her own mind; you certainly have my permission. Now tell me about India." Mom chalked up her dad's ease with his future son-in-law's surprising request to good parenting. She explained:

> I had been making good decisions in my life and he trusted me. He'd done the work of a parent and then set me free.
>
> I've always been adventurous, even more so in some ways than Dick, perhaps a trait I inherited from my father. When I was a kid, my dad took me hunting with him; I was there when he shot deer and dressed them and also accompanied him on many fishing outings. Of course Dick's decision to spend two years in India was a risky adventure of faith, a decision which I admired.

Mom says she was not intimidated by the prospect of being a pastor's wife. "My faith came alive for me those two years at UPC, so I really was interested in serving some way in the church. I never felt the call to go to seminary myself, so this fit."

Growing up in Yakima, Washington, Mom attended church with her parents Dick and Grace, sister Joan and brother Kim at a

Disciples of Christ church. The church was focused on preaching good works and supported missionaries in their work throughout the world. Mom spoke of the vivid stories she had heard as a child from missionaries who excited her sense of adventure. For instance she remembers one missionary who came back from the heart of Africa telling stories of tribes that had rituals like plunging the arm of a person suspected of lying into a pot of boiling oil to determine if they were being truthful or not. If the arm emerged without being withered, the person was cleared of the allegation.

While Mom's parents were moral, responsible and loving people, they were two different personalities—a confident, sporty, country-raised Dad and a cultured, sophisticated but less secure, city-girl Mom. My mom grew up with a lot of love but not peace. There was much bickering in her home. The church they attended didn't foster a sense of peace either, focusing instead on the need to do good works as a way to be Christian and earn God's love. By the time Mom got to college and started attending UPC and Bible studies, she wasn't rebelling or looking for anything specific but knew the moment her faith became real for her:

> I regularly attended Earl's Bible class for college kids on Sunday mornings. During Easter Season one Sunday we were discussing John 20:1-18 but what struck me were verses 14-16. When the risen Jesus addresses Mary as "Woman," she thinks he is the gardener, but when he calls her "Mary," she immediately knows it is Jesus. It struck me then that Jesus knows me by name—what a wonderful expression of God's love for me! For many years I could not talk about this passage without crying because it meant so much to me.

For Mom it was a confirmation that God knew her and loved her, evidence of God's grace in her life. It was a flip of the paradigm that she had heard growing up, so that instead of doing good works to earn God's love and acceptance, she felt that she was already loved and accepted by God and so was therefore inspired to live a life of service. Hearing a Biblical scholar give a talk, she was taken by a description of the purpose of studying the Bible: it will ring true to the needs of your heart. That passage rang true to Mom's heart, infusing her with the warmth of a grace-filled life, guided by a personal relationship with God through Jesus.

My mom was planning a December wedding. Dad could begin his final year at Princeton Seminary in September and she would join him after the wedding in December. She had received a fellowship for graduate study at UW and had already laid out a course of study toward a Masters Degree in Russian Studies with Dr. Donald Treadgold, a highly regarded professor whom she revered. Then my dad started advocating for a September wedding: "We could go back together to Princeton right now. I have a friend there who could find us a place to live and we'd have the whole year together instead of six months!"

Mom debated the pros and cons of wedding dates, pointing out things that were important to her, such as having time for wedding showers with family and friends and being concerned that her sister, Joan, who volunteered to make her wedding dress, wouldn't have time to do it. Also Mom had six attendants who needed to get their dresses made. She felt rushed! But they were married by Earl Palmer at University Presbyterian Church on Sunday afternoon, September 17, 1961, a full six weeks after they got engaged and three months after they met! Now my mom says with a chuckle, "You know what, I felt rushed our entire marriage! So, he was showing me what he was like up front, right then."

In that short time, though, they had figured out that their values and beliefs aligned. Dad finished his devotion, "The Lord's Internal Exam," with a life lesson that I think he learned from his marriage.

> Have you seen the latest statistics on cosmetic surgery in our country? They are on the upswing exponentially!!
>
> In our fast moving and competitive society, we are told that it is what is on the outside that impresses people the most. To be strong (like a horse) and quick (like a warrior) scores big time. In romantic attachments, it is the "cute and fun" in someone else that draws us to them. We are a "cosmetic" culture—if we can make a good external appearance we think we will go a long way.
>
> Not so with the Lord. He looks on the heart, remember David! His concern is what is going on inside us rather than just how we look on the outside. And there are two qualities named here that provide a good beginning to this internal exam:
>
> Those who fear him! This does not mean we simply quake before the Lord, it has more to do with deep wonder, respect and awe. To fear the Lord is to take God seriously, to know that we have all come from him and we will all return to him, and our relationship with him ought to command serious attention! The opposite of "fear" of the Lord would be crass indifference!
>
> Those who put their hope in his unfailing love! Hope is a much stronger word in the Bible

than it is in our daily speech. We might hope that the Cats never lose a game ... knowing all the time that they will. We use 'hope' for things that we doubt will ever happen. In the Bible, hope was a word of confidence and trust, an assurance of things not seen but which we believe are certain and reliable ... things like the "unfailing love of the Lord!"

We would all be wise to think more deeply about what impresses us in life and in others. For someone to be "strong and quick" or "cute and fun" is not enough for the long haul in a relationship. We need someone who takes God seriously and who lives a life confident in God's unfailing love. Those qualities will endure ... forever!

This devotion reminds me of the question that my parents always asked about new friends. Do they go to church? They asked that so often that I completely disregarded it. I didn't go to church so how relevant could that question be? But as I've experienced what meditation and spiritual practice have done for me, I found the translation that applies to my life. On what resources and habits will we fall back when life gets hard? It's so easy to be nice and charming when all is going well, but it's a better predictor of how we will behave to understand the tool set we are working on building every day of every week. In any long relationship, it's not a matter of if we will hurt each other but when, so what practices do we have to forgive and be forgiven?

Margie and Dick, circa 1939

Helen and Doug come for Parents' Weekend, 1956

ASUW President, 1956-1957

Dick crossing Khyber Pass, 1959

The Indian experience, 1959-1961

Carolyn and Dick married in 1961

The Leon family in the Philippines, 1975

Dick with lifelong friends, Kathy and Dale Bruner, 1995

Dick's last Sunday as Senior Pastor,
Bellevue Presbyterian Church, 2001

Dick and Scott Dudley, 2005

Carolyn and Dick, Priest Lake, ID, 2002

Dick, Carolyn and Wynne at Camp Muir
on Mount Rainier, 2000

Wynne at the base of Khumbu Icefall, Everest Base Camp, 2001

Wynne and Indigo on the Summit of Mt. Adams, 2009

Wynne, Carolyn and Dick on favorite walk at Discovery Park, 2013

Carolyn and Dick, Roche Harbor, 2013

TWELVE

*A Dose of Reality by Dick Leon, Daily Devotions,
January, 2011, Volume 38, Number 1,
Northminster Presbyterian Church, Tucson, AZ*

*Have mercy on me, O God, according to your unfailing love;
according to your great compassion blot out my transgressions.
Wash away all my iniquity and cleanse me from my sin.
For I know my transgressions, and my sin is always before me.
Against you, you only, have I sinned and done what is evil
in your sight, so that you are proved right when you speak
and justified when you judge. Psalm 51:1-4*

HONOR AND RESPONSIBILITY ARE TWO THEMES THAT Dad mentioned often in our conversations about faith. At the end of "Healing, If We Want It" he wrote, "Jesus offers us wholeness and wellness. But we have to want it and all the joys, obligations and responsibilities that come with being fit." In our conversations together, he said, "To follow an honorable path, to live an honorable life has its own self reward. With regard to this not being the only life and the only world, that'd be nice [a nice reward]. But it's not necessary in order to live an honorable life now. It's the smart thing to do." I had a feeling that my concept of honor and responsibility were missing the depth he intended by those statements. Is responsibility just doing what you say you'll do and keeping obligations? Is honor limited to behaving according to the Ten Commandments? There is some aspect of spiritual obedience that he referred to obliquely in conjunction with those two ideas that went over my head until I had a particular experience in meditation class that enlightened me.

In meditation classes we expanded the repertoire from just breathing and a little yoga to doing audio or visual exercises. It was through a visual exercise that I began to realize how present my inner narrator was, how much it was guiding my experience and even my physical reactions. In this particular exercise, we closed our eyes and listened to this narrative:

> Imagine you are on a bus going through Guatemala City. It is a hot day, in the nineties and all the windows are open, there is no air conditioning. You are standing in the middle of the bus as it stops and a family gets on, the woman carrying a case of chickens that she stores in the rack above your head. As the bus leaves that stop, it ends up in a traffic jam caused by a car that has toppled a cart carrying papaya so you are idling as it sounds as if every single car around you is honking their horn and the exhaust comes pouring in the window. Finally, you move again but at the next stop, so many people get on that the aisle is now clogged and people press against you from all sides. The man next to you smells as if he hasn't bathed in a week.

Oh, my goodness, I was near to panicking at this point in the meditation. I could feel my pulse accelerate and my senses became overwhelmed. It could be a scene directly from one of Dad's letters in India where he describes a train ride: "We took the 14 hour train ride to Serampore, twenty miles north to Calcutta. What a mob for the train. We traveled third class. As we waited we noticed a huge mass of people sitting on the train platform with us. As the train came we stood and soon found ourselves amidst a pushing, crawling, crowding throng attempting to squeeze into a three-foot opening. Jim got ahead and made it in, I found my American victory spirit catching me up in the fight."

Back in meditation class, we continued our visualization exercise:

> Now picture yourself sitting on a river bank of a lazily moving river. The water is a rich green but very clear to the bottom. It is midafternoon and you are shaded by a nice canopy of high trees so that there are a few patches of sunlight that stream down but the temperature is perfect with a slight breeze. You are watching a water skimmer move across the water in a balletic fashion and a chorus of frogs and birds is all around you. You lie back and feel the mossy bank of the river support your back as you inhale the sweet smell of jasmine that comes on the breeze.

Aaahhh. My physical reaction slowed immediately as the narrative in my head changed. We finished the meditation practice:

> You are by the river and you take that calm that is with you, it is in your center, it deepens with every breath and you imagine yourself in that bus again. Keep the calm center of the river as you no-

> tice everything around you, the noises, the smells, the sounds. Just observe the sensations of the bus, but don't attach to any one thing. If you start to lose the calm, close your eyes and imagine the river, how the people around you are a chorus of their own, maybe not too different from the frogs.

I found that I could hold the calm in the meditation practice as the story reframed and I realized in the moment how much my head was manipulating me. Dad did much the same as he was finishing the train ride:

> ... then I realized that it was silly to fight to only end up standing anyway as there couldn't be any seats left by then. So I relaxed and let the mob push, which they did, and ended up standing, watching and being watched as all the other 3rd classers anxiously pushed by to fill the full aisles. On the way back we were able to get one luggage rack to sleep on so I let Jim take first shift; I had only the floor left to stand, sit or lie as I pleased. I drew many glances and glares of surprise, some of disgust, as I would huddle up on the floor next to our brown skinned brethren. Many would try to converse and we'd usually end up laughing as I'd pull out my Hindi practice sheets and work on the alphabet. One could speak some English, so he sat next to me and with wide eyes asked what I was doing on the floor "in all this dirt?"

Dad didn't have the language skills to explain why he was on the floor, so he lobbed the question back at the gentleman, asking why he was in the dirt. Dad couldn't understand his response.

Finally, they came to understand that at the very least, they didn't understand; it became a joke between them. He finished:

> Then we worked on some Hindi together and between his thanks and praises we actually made progress. The Indians take it as a great compliment to know what we are doing and most are especially excited to see us learning their language.

One morning shortly after meditation class, I found myself looking into the refrigerator. Sour cream? Leftover pasta? I wanted to find something good to coat Biscuit's daily medications. I reasoned that he must be bored with the peanut butter I was using to give him the medication. But then I stilled and just listened to the narrative in my head. It told me that I was feeling sorry for Biscuit as I looked at the leftovers. Still standing there, I looked over at Biscuit, who was lying there carefree just like every other day. I slowly shut the refrigerator and fed him the pills in peanut butter. He didn't hesitate for a second to take them. I had had zero basis for feeling sorry for him because he was bored, making up a story that involved that emotion and then starting to act on it. This realization fascinated me as if I had just been told a new law of the universe and perhaps it was, the law of wasting energy based on an emotion that was extended due to a false story line.

Hilarious, I thought to myself, but then I started to notice how often I did it. There is a three-story square house in my neighborhood that I see every morning when I'm walking Biscuit. It never has the shades drawn, and in the winter, when it's still dark outside, the occupants seem to have every room lit so it looks like a cut away where you can see the evidence of life lived in every room, books stacked here, a sweater thrown over a chair there and the father, in his robe, going out to get the paper. It gives me a sense of family, community and closeness, yet I've never met these neighbors. Emotions are typically felt for 90 seconds, but Pema Chödrön suggests that it is when we create stories around them that we make them last much longer. Once aware, I found I was doing that often, usually with happy and warm stories that I liked. I would walk into my own home and smell ginger snaps that I had just baked and taken out of the oven to cool. Made from a recipe brought home from junior high home economics class, the cookies' aroma made me hook into the story of warmth, tradition and goodness.

Once I was aware of all the storylines that were occupying my mind and emotions, I began to see references made by many of my favorite authors about the phenomena. In our conversations on the topic, Dad referred to it as the "tyranny of the self." Often harmless when reminding us of the feelings we value, it can lull us into thinking as narrators. We hold the truth and we can then be destructive when we use our story to determine our course of action instead of allowing God to, especially in unhappy storylines of ego, revenge, or unfairness. While discussing meditation with an acquaintance, she told me about Dr. Jill Bolte Taylor and a TED talk. Soon, I found my favorite description of the brain's processes in Dr. Taylor's book, *My Stroke of Insight*.

Dr. Taylor, a neuroanatomist, was 37 years old when she experienced a massive stroke that for a time wiped out the operation of the left hemisphere of her brain. It was then that she experienced what she calls Nirvana. She describes the right brain as a parallel processor that perceives the fabric of the moment we are in, the sensations and the connections between ourselves and what we are experiencing. The left brain functions as the organizing engine; it is sequencing, recognizing patterns and categorizing and through the language centers located there, creating a sense of self. The left brain, with those language centers, is also responsible for what Dr. Taylor describes as "brain chatter."

For most healthy people, both hemispheres work in concert most of the time, but when Dr. Taylor experienced her stroke, she lost the function of her left brain in large part and had to work for seven years to restore its function. Throughout this journey, she experienced the beauty and peace of the right brain and realized how much of a choice we make in perceiving our experience, almost always unconsciously. We can choose to involve our right brain more actively in each experience to bring in peace and connectedness to the situation.

As I worked to quiet the brain chatter and meditate into the silence, I started to unravel one of Dad's sayings, a favorite quote from John Calvin, "The powers of self-delusion are unlimited." The risk, Dad said, is of people looking for guidance from within themselves when the self, the narrator, is more broken and out of order than one thinks. The introspection is too self-centered and too self-serving and one ends up deluding oneself and creating a world view on the basis of nothing more than our skewed perception or wishes.

I dated a man in my twenties whom I loved deeply. I met him on a warm August Saturday night at a crowded party thrown by one of my sorority sisters from college. The attraction was instantaneous. He was handsome, smart, athletic and funny and I couldn't believe he was looking at me that way! I don't think I talked to a single other person at the party that night; no one else mattered. He called on Tuesday and we spent all night on the phone together. Soon we went out for Italian food and were holding hands by the time we went to the bar around the corner, not wanting the evening to be over.

We connected, we laughed, giggled, watched the *X-Files* and *Mad About You,* moved in together, adopted a kitten, bought our first brand new car. We talked about getting married and having daughters, tall and leggy, just like him, but in the back of my mind, I couldn't get over the fact that the beginning of our relationship was messy and that was all my fault. I had been seeing someone else when I met him, someone about whom I thought I should be serious. So I had overlapped the relationships for the first three months or so, causing a lot of anxiety in myself and others. The man I loved had a friend who simply hated me for the pain I caused him in those early months when I was still seeing both guys, and she was an ongoing reminder of my lack of character. This created a tension in me that built up over the two years we were together until I was impatient and judgmental. Finally, one night as we drove home on a deserted freeway after a brutally long day, he made a grumpy comment, not directed at me but something along the lines of working too hard for The Man. I thought, "That's it, I'm done. We have completely different attitudes so this won't work," and I broke up with him. It was a load of bull but I had my story and went with it, never admitting, not even to myself, that it was because of all that I had done wrong at the beginning of the relationship; I feared I deserved to be hurt because of my actions. Instead I made it out to be because we weren't a good match. I could have uncovered my delusion when he found a therapist and we went to three sessions of couples counseling, but I was not open to the introspection, likely fearing what it would uncover in me. I created a delusion that I thought reflected better on me and one where breaking up wasn't my fault.

It seems so simple in the retelling, but at the time I really needed to buy into my delusion. Most of the internal tension dissipated with the breakup, but it left a little residue of dissonance that meant I started looking forward to that second (or more) glass of wine at night and didn't sleep as well. I honestly didn't see the true reason for the breakup or the delusion I created until I started meditating. Then I saw some of my patterns in a truthful but non-judgmental way and connected the dots to the heartbreak I caused myself and others. I had apologized to both men over the years; they had both moved on and it was of no consequence to them, but without acknowledging my true failing I couldn't forgive myself.

Dad finishes his devotion, "A Dose of Reality," referring to the verses from Psalms and an explanation of why a dose of reality is good for the soul:

> Have these kinds of thought been yours lately? Have you heard anyone else express such thoughts about their "sins and iniquities?"
>
> These words are jarring to our ears because we live in a culture that wants us to feel good about ourselves. 'Self-esteem' is the code word for us all today. So, any talk of "sin" or "iniquity" or having "done evil" is hard to swallow! The power of this Psalm is that it presents us with a hard dose of reality about our sinfulness.
>
> The title of a recent book describes our culture well: *The Narcissism Epidemic*. Narcissism is excessive self-love, which in the extreme means we have to deny the dark side in our lives. It is popular, but unhealthy!
>
> Here is the irony of it all: Only when we see our "iniquities" can we be freed of them. Our culture tells us we can be free of our faults by deny-

> ing them, the gospel calls us to name them and entrust them, and ourselves, to the "mercy of God and his unfailing love."

Entrusting ourselves to the mercy of God is such a lofty idea that I need to boil it down to a human level. I found in Dad's letters from India that during the most difficult times, he had a pattern of confession, prayer and then realization of grace. His confessions, so funny to me knowing Dad, are most often of impatience, "The greatest need for me besides love . . . is patience. Just today at lunch while listening to a new friend I realized another source of impatience, which is best illustrated by Hindi movies which take three hours to tell a 15-30 minute story." He would describe his remedy, "I have run, crept or forced myself into the quiet of prayer, of reading Bonhoeffer, Pascal or Paul and reflection." And he would write of the beauty of grace, "What pain comes when I think over these days and the loveless times, yet what encouragement when I happen on to these evidences of grace when in spite of it all I felt love."

Dad made things like forgiveness and grace seem so effortless, but he also spent a whole career focusing on examples, not only in Jesus' life but in countless others like Nelson Mandela and, in some of my favorite stories, sports figures. He admired the Seattle Seahawks for recruiting a player even after they discovered he had a heart problem, cutting him after he joined so he would have pay and health benefits. He would talk about the standing ovation that Ichiro received when returning to play the Seattle Mariners after he'd joined the NY Yankees because he had left gracefully. Or this example he included in a 2010 sermon:

> I was reading my weekly theological journal the other day, *Sports Illustrated*, and it carried a

great story about James Joyce, not the author, but the baseball umpire who stole Galaragga's perfect game by blowing the call at first base for what should have been the last out of the game! But here is the best part of the story. Joyce looked at the tape, realized he was wrong, apologized and asked to be forgiven! Have you ever known an umpire or referee to do that? So when he walked onto the field for the next night's game, he was given a standing ovation by the home fans in Detroit and Galaragga himself gave Joyce the lineup at home plate as a public gesture of his forgiveness!

Forgiveness and grace were the two cornerstones of Dad's beliefs, not fire and brimstone. I got a shiver every time he told me the story of *Les Miserables* so I asked him to tell it to me again. In his eyes, the story shows that the only force that can change us is grace. We don't change because of laws or being told what not to do, but through grace we can learn to become responsible and honorable:

> The turning point of Victor Hugo's masterpiece occurs when Jean Valjean gets out of prison; the poor guy is marked forever, can't get a job and is struggling. A priest sees him and welcomes him into his home. He feeds him because he's starving and gives him overnight lodging. But Jean Valjean is fundamentally a thief; he steals silverware from the priest and gets caught. The policemen bring him back to the priest and say, "We've caught the thief. He's stolen your goods. He'll go to prison forever. All you need to do is lay charges against

him." And the priest counters, "Oh, no, he didn't steal those, those I gave him and besides, Jean Valjean, I forgot to give you the candlesticks." That act of grace changes him forever. It is the turning point in his life. And all the way through the play, the candlesticks keep appearing. In the book of Revelation, when John has a vision, he sees Jesus in all of His magnificence walking among the candlesticks which he says represent the church, the Christian community, the people of faith who live by grace and sustain life at its best.

But Dad didn't just tell stories of forgiveness and grace, he learned to live his life with those characteristics at his core. As an adult, fortunately, there have been fewer occasions for which I need forgiveness from my parents. But in 2014 I went with friends to stay overnight and hike on Mt. Rainier, and my parents were nice enough to stay with my animals that night. We intended to climb to Camp Muir on Friday and then have breakfast and come home mid-day on Saturday. Except, the weather was terrible on Friday, so we took a short hike and scrapped the plan to go to Camp Muir. But it was beautiful the next morning so we changed our minds again and headed up after breakfast. I had no cell phone coverage in the park so I didn't text or call about the change of plans, and then my phone died about a half hour into the hike while taking the first picture of the day.

I've hiked to Camp Muir dozens of times. It's not trivial because it's hiking from 5,400 feet to 10,200 feet, but it's not technical and if you are in decent shape, it's just a matter of sticking with it. We didn't return to the parking lot until 5pm, didn't get back to Seattle until 8pm. I saw a pay phone in the restrooms on Mt. Rainier and for a second considered calling but couldn't even remember if I had a calling card any more.

My parents had stayed overnight with the animals and then returned to their home. When I didn't call by 3pm, it was a little odd, by 5pm a little worrisome, but by 8pm it was just short of panic. My parents knew I wouldn't leave my animals that long and that it was unthinkable I didn't call in the age of cell phones. They trusted that I was experienced but it's a mountain with 26 glaciers and there are fatalities on the mountain usually every year. Each fatality is widely reported in the Pacific Northwest.

When I finally got home from the Muir trip a little after 8 pm, I heard the worry in my mom's voice when I reached her and it was heart breaking. I made one little mistake after another that led to something that was unnecessarily stressful on them when they were doing me a favor. I felt terrible!

My dad made a joke of how surprising it must be to me that I had to report in to my parents when I was in my 40's. Then he said, "It's okay, we forgive you." That was it. He didn't amplify the hurt, use it as an excuse not to watch the pets in the future or leverage it in any way. It was done. It felt like what forgiveness should really be, my true confession, no excuses and my dad's loving absolution.

Inspired by Dad, but needing a more tangible way to start working on forgiveness, not only of others but of myself, I began practicing the Loving Kindness meditation.

I find a comfortable seat, with my hips higher than my knees, comfortable and stable. Closing my eyes, I picture someone toward whom I have really warm feelings. I see them right in front of me and I breathe in and think "May I be happy" and breathe out and think "May you be happy" as if I were saying it to the person I am imagining. My feeling of happiness in this context is not gaiety or momentary satisfaction but deep contentedness. Then I breathe in and say "May I be at peace" and breathe out and think "May you be at peace." I believe this is peace, not from lack of conflict, but from freedom of inner struggle. Finally I breathe in and think "May I be loved" and breathe out and think "May you be loved." This is love stemming from a genuine connection with all beings.

Then I imagine someone toward whom I don't have an emotional reaction one way or the other, perhaps the grocery store clerk or person in the car next to mine this morning and picture them in front of me, and I repeat the same exercise, wishing them happiness, peace and love.

Finally, I pick someone with whom I have unresolved or negative feelings that I need to soften and let go. I picture them in front of me and repeat the same exercise, wishing them happiness, peace and love.

Each time I created an openness in myself for forgiveness and grace. The added dimension of responsibility, I came to believe, was finding a way to be internally honest, guided by Divine truth, not my own narrator. Honor, it seems, includes practicing forgiveness and grace.

THIRTEEN

Worthiness *by Dick Leon, Daily Devotions, May, 2011, Volume 38, Number 5, Northminster Presbyterian Church, Tucson, AZ*

"... so that you may live a life worthy of the Lord and please him in every way: bearing fruit in every good work, growing in the knowledge of God..." Col 1:10

BLAISE PASCAL WAS DAD'S FAVORITE PHILOSOPHER, A 17th Century mathematician and inventor of the syringe, the barometer and the autobus. That list makes me giggle, the syringe AND the autobus? But Dad swore it's true even as he would laugh and say, "Really, I'm serious." In one of his letters home from India, he quoted Blaise Pascal, "The strength of a man's virtue must not be measured by his efforts but by his ordinary life." And so after their quick courtship, my parents embarked on their ordinary life together.

During the Christmas break of Dad's last year at Princeton, 1961, Gary Demarest asked Dad to join him as Assistant Pastor at Hamburg Presbyterian Church. Dad had offers to come back to Seattle as well, but he thought that seemed too easy. He was well known and he could possibly just rely on the relationships he had already established. He was unknown in Hamburg and felt the need to go there to see what he could do without riding on his reputation. Gary was a great companion and mentor to Dad and his wife Marily was a supportive friend and role model to Mom, so Dad accepted the position to start in September of 1962. Dad described Hamburg, NY at the time as "a sleepy little village, very friendly and quaint." The economic engine of the area came from Bethlehem Steel. This was the first of what would be four churches in Dad's career, Hamburg Presbyterian, Union Church of Manila, First Presbyterian Church of Spokane and Bellevue Presbyterian.

After eight years in Hamburg, Dad took a position in the Philippines as Senior Pastor of the Union Church of Manila, an English-speaking, interdenominational, multinational Christian congregation, a position that he would hold for six years. Earl and Shirley Palmer played a part in this choice, recommending my father for the church in the Philippines after they had served there for six years. My parents felt deeply that this was God's calling and felt confident they were on the right path, believing that pastors should move to a new church every eight to twelve years. They remained confident even after Ferdinand Marcos declared martial law about two years into our time there. Mom and Dad met Ferdinand and Imelda at their daughter, Imee (Maria Imelda Josefa Romualdez-Marcos) Marcos' high school graduation. Imee attended the same school that we did and when the seniors voted on the speaker for their graduation, Ferdinand came in first and Dad came in second, so Ferdinand gave the commencement speech and Dad performed the invocation. My mom recounted how she asked Marcos to scoot in for a picture before the event and Dad told how he accidentally put his hand on a gun carried by one of Ferdinand's security detail when he slapped him on the back to say, "Hi," trying to be friendly, but neither was arrested so perhaps their faith was well-placed.

Dad's third pastorate was the First Presbyterian Church in Spokane, Washington. My parents were ready to be nearer to their families and wanted their kids to go to high school in the States. In the ten years that Dad was Senior Pastor there, the membership of the church doubled from around 900 to 1,800. He focused on creating a vital experience for people and their children. It was a comprehensive ministry, covering a whole range of personal faith, children's ministry, adult care, and outreach. Other churches had left the city and moved to the suburbs but Dad and his staff said, "We are committed to staying downtown and serving the city." When Bloomsday started [a running race launched in Spokane in 1977], we had a t-shirt, "The church with the city in its heart." Dad reveled in being a Husky in Cougar country as he often said, a University of Washington (Husky) graduate in the heartland of the intra-state rival, Washington State University (Cougar).

In 1986, after 10 years in Spokane and after receiving his Doctor of Ministry degree from San Francisco Theological Seminary in 1982, Dad moved to his fourth church, Bellevue Presbyterian in Bellevue, Washington. He described this church as an edge city church, a city that is on the edge of a big city but has a lot of growth in and of itself. Full of members that were highly educated, type A personalities, captains of industry, Dad described this as a ministry that once again tried to reach people where they were. But with people who were intellectually, physically, financially and professionally very successful, the need for God was sometimes less evident and harder to cultivate. It was an effective ministry as evidenced by the membership growth of the church from 1,200 to 2,500 during his tenure. Overall, it was a wonderful culmination of his ministry: a classic suburban church in Hamburg, an international church in the Philippines with an inter-denominational congregation, a downtown church in Spokane where they could tend to the community in which they were directly located, and then finally Bellevue Presbyterian Church where the focus was on directing the fruits of success to the mission of God. In all churches, Dad described the central purpose as serving family issues, encouraging all to reach out to the community, city and world beyond, and most importantly, loving people. These three themes stood out as the pillars of his life throughout our conversations: family, social action and love.

Neither of my parents had come from families with healthy interactions. While my dad's parents were very affectionate with each other, there was a complete lack of discussion of anything serious or meaningful as far as my dad observed. My mom, on the other hand, described her parents' marriage as one where they didn't have good ways of communicating and working out their differences, spending little time with each other but a lot of individual time with the kids. Mom had a lot of outdoors time with her dad and intensive piano studies with her mom. Mom and Dad chose to live in a place farther away from their families so they could create their own patterns. Yet there were many times when my Dad was working all the time that Mom felt very lonely and longed for family to be closer.

When Gary left for La Canada Presbyterian Church in 1965, Hamburg Presbyterian Church called my dad to stay on and be senior pastor. He was 30 years old, three years out of seminary, the church had about 1,000 members and he worked too hard, as my mom knows better than anyone! Mom remembered this as a difficult time:

> Dad was gone all the time and I remember being very lonely and I would never, because of

> pride, be able to call my mom and say "I'm really lonely" and intimate that things weren't working very well with my marriage because I was so determined to do better. I had no one to turn to because in the church everybody is your employer. I felt that there was no way I could tell anybody that I thought Dick was working too hard and I didn't like what they were demanding of him.

One of Dad's insecurities stemmed from the impression that pastors only work on Sundays and as a young pastor of a large congregation Dad felt the weight of all the work and expectations. He said, "During our Hamburg years I would have been the most insecure." Mom recalled, with a chuckle that hindsight had afforded, one of his habits caused by that insecurity – he would never answer the phone when he was home because people had the stereotype that a pastor only works on Sunday and if they ever caught him at home, even if it was his day off, people would actually make corny jokes, like, "You only have to work on Sunday" when he was working his tail off. Dad had a very clear memory of a woman from the church coming by their house in Hamburg one Friday, his day off, and he was there. She said to him, "'Oh, what are you doing home?" And he felt as if he'd just died inside.

Mom described the tension of those early years when she was competing with God's work. Fortunately, her strong belief in the church fostered a reaction that was a lot more gracious than mine as a kid:

> It was hard to talk about things when there is no easy resolution. So if the main thing I wanted to say to Dick was, "You are working too hard. I need you home more," then he's in a bind because

he's feeling overloaded with so many responsibilities, how can he turn his back on them?

We found it hard to talk about things in small enough steps so that they could be changed or corrected. It would have been better to find a beginning place and to say that it hurts me when such and such happens. Then we might have been able to talk about one specific issue and maybe we could have done that differently. That would have been better than saying or implying your whole profession needs to go out the window. We didn't have good tools to work with at that time in our marriage.

By the time they moved to the Philippines, the loneliest periods of Mom and Dad's marriage were behind them. The anger she had felt when isolated in Hamburg had started to resolve as she gained more time to follow her pursuits because of the household help they had there. The anger had started a cycle where Dad retreated because of his inexperience with conflict, thus resulting in more isolation and that cycle was thankfully broken. Mom and Dad got better at communication and began the pattern of participating in small groups, which helped when they couldn't communicate directly. While she still felt that she needed to protect his reputation because he was a leader in the church, she felt she could be more open in small groups that she trusted. Within these groups of four or five couples, they talked, prayed and worked on the issues of life. Often our social activities were determined by these small groups so I also benefitted from the support and love of these tight-knit alliances. Even when their kids were grown, Dad had retired, and Mom and Dad had fewer pressures of life, they persisted in this practice as a way to continue finding vitality and depth of experience, the most recent small group being five couples from the Sammamish Presbyterian Church that continue to support our family life even as it is redefined with Dad's death.

The second pillar of Dad's life, social action, had deep roots stemming from his time in India but flourished throughout his career and possibly bloomed most visibly in his retirement. As a young man in a country that was adjusting its societal structures as the caste system was outlawed and was emerging as a new force in the world, Dad wondered how his two-year experience would affect what he did with his life. A letter to his family friends, the Rutledges, detailed these ponderings:

> I am becoming aware of how narrow the Western normal education is today by limiting its studies to the road from Athens, Greece to Washington D.C., especially when over two-thirds of the world is now living in the Eastern tradition and is no longer sleeping in innocent submission to the West. Much of this is why we are here; the next question, however, which [we] are only now beginning to face, is what these years will mean for our future. It will be no easy task to simply return to the comforts and blindness of the rich American way in two years while having impressed in our minds the many, many problems, material, moral and spiritual, that this new world faces.

As he embarked on his career, Dad seemed to relish getting involved in what he saw as the Christian mission, fighting for the poor and oppressed: "It seems every year I was pushing for some social issue that made our more conservative people mad at me."

The social turmoil of the 60's had brought their share of tensions to Hamburg. He recalled being in support of Open Housing and serving on the board of Friendship House, a social service agency in Lackawanna, a predominantly industrial city near Hamburg. Mom marched with some of her friends from the church in an Open Housing parade. Because of their involvement with Friendship House, they met Saul Alinsky, the community organizer said to have inspired Barack Obama and Hilary Clinton. They hosted him for a dinner with friends. Mom thinks one of the reasons that it was a relief to move to the Philippines was not to be involved every year with social issues that were just tearing everyone apart. Except that Saul Alinsky, or at least his organization, followed them there as well.

In the early 1970's in the Philippines, Saul Alinsky had an organizational team to try to help ZOTO, the Zone One Tondo Organization, learn how to protest. The Union Church of Manila had always been involved in Tondo, one of the poorest sections of Manila, so Dad joined the board of a mission hospital in Tondo. People Power was the word of the day and one of the first strategies was to have some kind of initial victory to build upon. Culturally it was difficult for Filipinos to confront someone directly. Alinsky's strategy seemed to be to protest against someone that they thought would be an easy target, and since Union Church was already on their side, it became their first object lesson. They wanted the church to sign a pledge of support and some kind of protest against the government.

Dad was having a hard time getting the Church Council to sign on to Alinsky's pledge. After it was proposed but before the church could agree to it, a group from Alinsky's organization came to church. As soon as they appeared, one of the head ushers, a retired

California police officer, closed a corridor gate to keep them out.

He rushed to tell Dad, "All of these people from Zone One are here and they are coming to worship and I've kept them out behind the gate."

"No, open the gate, let them in, this is a worship service, let them in." Dad replied.

He described the scene that ensued:

> One guy from their group sat in the front row with his Bible open the whole time and I thought, "I am sure he has planned some kind of protest in the middle of my sermon and I've got to figure out in advance how I'm going to handle it." But, he never budged through the whole service, I have no idea why. Of course, he didn't need to because he made me nervous enough without saying anything.

The protest then spilled over to the following week.

> They came and marched around the outside of the sanctuary with huge signs. Through our large glass windows we could look out and see, "Leon is an Ugly American" and "Leon is a Liar." Then the protestors got back on their bus and went home. There was no real confrontation. We ended up signing the document because we were obviously on their side and trying to support their cause.

None of this deterred Mom and Dad from their dedication to social action. In the late 1970's and early 1980's, Dad participated in the creation of CAN, Christian Aid Network, uniting Spokane churches of all denominations in common service to needy people. He developed a partnership with a black church in the 1980's so they could stand up against White Supremacy Sunday. In the 1990's, while rebuilding the Bellevue Presbyterian Church, he rallied for space in the church to house the Eastside Academy for high school drop-outs to give them a second chance. In retirement, Mom and Dad went to Botswana with Habitat for Humanity, mixing and pouring cement in sweltering heat. Throughout these years my mom maintained a steady passion and interest in the Soviet Union and Russia where they visited for the first time in 1974, then led short-term mission groups there from the Bellevue Church between the years of 1994 and 2001. Mom went back to the University of Washington in the 1990's and received a second degree, this one in Russian Language and Literature and in 1994 taught English in Moscow for five weeks.

Like small groups, social action was a commitment that Dad maintained until his death. After a trip to Israel in 2013, Mom and Dad became involved in the pursuit of justice for Palestinians, both Christians and Muslims, a cause that led him to become the chairman of the board of Kairos USA just before his death. Dad understood how sensitive this cause was and yet still was brave enough to broach the subject in sermons and classes at Bellevue Presbyterian Church and Sammamish Presbyterian Church. In a sermon he delivered in June, 2013 at Bellevue Presbyterian, he started with a caveat to introduce the story:

> *I need a side-bar here to keep from getting into deep trouble with this story. I want to affirm that there are good political reasons to be a staunch supporter of Israel. However, I do not believe Israel has a divine right to the whole land so they can treat their neighbors badly! This story of Daoud Nassar shows a great injustice but I don't want you to go*

away thinking I am trying to make a political statement. If possible, I want to use this story for the personal issue of how Daoud's faith helps him deal with his fears. OK?

Daoud's property is 100 acres of fertile land with abundant olive trees that provides his family with substantial income. But now Israel wants his land for one of their settlements. In 1991 the Israeli government declared the whole area including his property as "state property," even though it is located within the boundaries called the "West Bank" that the United Nations and subsequent peace treaties have identified as Palestinian Lands.

Daoud challenged this ruling by going to the Israeli courts with his ownership papers. He could prove that his family has owned this land for over 100 years, going back to the times of the Ottoman Empire. The court had never seen legal papers like this and didn't know what to do. So, now, 22 years later, the court has still refused to give a ruling. He has had to spend nearly $150,000 defending his property rights. While they live in this legal limbo, the Israel Defense Force (IDF) continues to make their life difficult. Several years ago the people in adjacent settlements came on his land and cut down 250 of his olive trees and the police did nothing about it.

The Army has blocked the main road into their property with huge boulders so everything has to be brought in by foot. They have had their electricity cut off, their water cut off and all requests for permits to build on the property denied.

At the same time, there are three huge Jewish Settlements surrounding his land with as many as 40,000 people and they all have full electricity, full access to running water and modern roads. When asked why they don't sell their property and move on, their response is telling. Daoud's brother, who helped give us a tour of their property, put it this way: "This land is our mother. We would never sell our mother!"

So, how has Daoud Nassar responded to the fear that their land and their existence could be taken away at any minute? I am so impressed to see his Christian spirit that enables him to persist on their land in spite of the oppressive tactics of Israel. This is Christian witness at its best. We sat with Daoud and he told us they will not live as victims and simply whine about their troubles. They are going to face their hardships and overcome them with new strategies for living.

One way they do this is by living in caves on the land since they cannot get a building permit to build homes. They collect rainwater in large cisterns to provide water for themselves and to irrigate their crops. (They've had to fight a demolition order on their cisterns, too.) They've built compost toilets. For electricity they have installed some solar panels. They were refused the use of a tractor to cultivate the land so they have planted a variety of crops by hand and with the help of internationals who have come from around the world to help them. They have set up a large tent (and they were given a demolition order on their tent as well) that serves as a dormitory for their international workers and this is why they've given their land the name "Tent of Nations." You can actually look them up on the web and read their story. With this help they have planted 1700 cabbage plants, 200 olive trees, more than a 1000 almond and plum trees.

And finally, they have shaped their lives around the simple but powerful line that is painted on a large stone at the entrance to their property: "WE REFUSE TO BE ENEMIES." This is a short paraprosdokian, did you notice? A paraprosdokian is a saying in which the last half is a surprise, often even humorous. For example: "Where there is a will ~ I want to be in it." Another, "War does not determine who is right ~ only who is left!" I like this one too, "I used to be indecisive ~ but now I'm not so sure." This is a good one if you disagree with someone, but I wouldn't recommend that you use it between a husband and wife! "If I agreed with you ~ we'd both be wrong!"

Well, Daoud's slogan also has a surprise ending: "We refuse ~ to be enemies!" You might expect it to say "We refuse to take your guff ... to accept your abuse ... or to let you abuse us ... or even, to be friends!" But no, he says we refuse to be enemies!

> So when the IDF come on their land to harass them, Daoud invites them in, has them sit at a table in one of their caves, serves them tea and asks how their family is. When he spoke with us he said we are not going to whine and play the role of victims. We are not going to let them turn us into enemies. We are human beings who can find ways to survive even with these limitations. And we will never resort to violence.

Dad seemed to get away with these calls to social action even as he irritated people because of the third pillar of his life and career: love. He loved people and as my brother Jay says, he met you where you were without leaving where he was. It was an ability that made him successful as a pastor, successful in life and also made him happy. When I probed him on the subject, he explained:

> Let's face it, everyone is on their own journey and we don't get to see everyone at the top of their game. Some are just getting started. We only get a glimpse of them at one point in time, some maybe longer, and our job is to love them so they move forward, closer to the Lord and closer to those God has placed in their lives.
>
> I've often kidded folks that when you start working with people, the first rule that you live with is, "People are weird." We are all weird, we are all funny combinations of funny stuff. So, what's that mean for us? How do you love people that are different in a weird sort of way? Well, you just try to help them, wherever they are. I mean, I never would have imagined, at 20 years old when

I finally made the decision to go in to ministry, I never would have thought that this is what my life would be like. I am so grateful to God for what that has meant, the number of lives that I've been able to be a part of. One of the unique things about ministry is that you are able to be with people in some of the most precious, important, holy moments of their life . . . birth, death, baptism, marriage, funeral, crisis. A pastor steps in to the middle of someone's life at those unique times and that is pretty rare.

In every church there is somebody that doesn't like me. But the root issue is relationships. When you love people and relate with them and they know you love them, you can get away with anything, a bad sermon, a missed call or what.

Mom had a unique vantage point for my dad's work and the love and relationships that he worked so hard at fostering. She observed:

> Not only did Dick have good content, good Biblical preaching that people were hungry for, but he also got to know people personally. He was warm and relational and people love that, plus he brought in good staff. Unlike many pastors, he liked administration which meant not only working with Session, the main body, but also all the committees that support the Session. That's why he was gone so many evenings because that's when committees met. Everything from mission to finance to Christian Ed, there is a committee

for every part of the church to make it work and he personally attended a lot of those meetings. I remember saying to Dick, "How can you stand one more meeting?" and he would say, "Well, I like the meetings. That's where you get to know the people closely and work with them."

His approach, as he explained it to me, was to work with people who wanted to be involved with the church to make sure that they had a meaningful task, they were rewarded and listened to and that they felt befriended. For someone who was going to be an elder for three years, he felt the right question to ask was, "At the end of the three years, do these people love the Lord, love the church and love their sense of ministry more than when you met them?" It's not "How do I put up with them for three years?" but "'How can I help them grow as people during their years?" For Dad, reframing the question changed the whole sense from merely existing to serving and befriending people. With each committee, elder, deacon or officer of the church, he knew he had a window into their life that he'd never have again and so it was best to love them through it!

It seems likely that he also earned some latitude for his positions on social causes by being very tolerant himself. Dad said that instead of always appointing people that agreed with him to permanent positions, such as in the Presbytery, he would also appoint people that he knew held different opinions and were perhaps more liberal. He loved the give and take and recognition of devoted, honest, faithful people that differed from him. Coming from a family home that avoided conflict, he steadily worked at dealing with adversity, assisted by the love of my mom, the support of small groups and his firm foundation of faith until he encouraged it, at least within the church.

While it's very true that Dad met people where they were and also loved them through it, he slipped in some encouragement for moving forward as well. Just as he did with me, with tennis, golf or moving forward from my divorce, he urged others to get moving. Jeanne Walsh, a neighbor in Spokane and Preschool Director at First Presbyterian of Spokane when Dad was Senior Pastor, recalled about Dad:

> He was such an amazing mix: generous with patience and with grace – and yet, "Let's get it done!" But I think we, as a couple and as a family, primarily experienced his grace ... his patience and his wisdom. As a staff member, I saw a lot of wisdom and compassion – a deep faith in God – as well as an ability and desire to get moving – and get us moving!! I remember watching him 'manage' people who inadvertently would attempt to 'take over' a meeting... and I observed him negotiate conflicts and strong personalities... I learned from him that a leader doesn't get to win every battle or win over every congregant. But he had a pretty good batting average, I thought, and an amazing understanding and acceptance of others.

Dad also loved "love" which was obvious in the laughter and twinkle when he told stories of the weddings he officiated. Throughout his career he performed 539 weddings, unusually high because he became a senior pastor at such a young age. While it could be tense at a wedding if there were family problems, he said overall, "Those moments were filled with much optimism and love within the families. They were a huge delight." Then he added, "Did I ever tell you about the bride who got sick?"

> This was in Spokane. The bride and her mother were estranged and when the mother showed up, the bride panicked. They stood out on the porch, she in her wedding gown trying to convince her mother not to come in. The mother did go away, but the bride was still emotionally on edge. During the wedding, she was white as a sheet. We got through the first part of the wedding just fine until she knelt down for prayer after the wedding vows. As she is kneeling down, she looks up at me and warns, "I can't hold it," and projectile vomits all over my shoes and robe. But we got through it without anybody in the congregation really knowing what happened. I had the best man step out back to bring a towel for the bride, I got Jan to play a little longer on the organ, and we got her cleaned up in time for the wedding kiss which probably wasn't very tasty, but nobody other than the immediate people up front knew what had happened.

In another memorable one that I witnessed as maid of honor, my friend Tracy's veil caught on fire after the lighting of the candles. After we had snuffed it out, Dad joked, "This marriage is on fire already!"

One of my favorites is the unity candle story. Dad explained:

> There are two candles on the altar which the mothers light before the service begins. Then later in the service the bride and groom light the unity candle from their two individual candles. In one ceremony, the bride steps back, takes her fingers

and snuffs out her husband's candle. I don't recall whether or not that marriage worked out. It was done in such jest, but things like that happen in a wedding and you can't do anything about it.

As we talked over the stories of his life, Dad reminisced:

Looking back on my life I see that it has been incredibly rich and good and diverse and full of gratification and challenge. I think of the time in Peru or India or in the Philippines, our times in Russia or the four churches we've pastored and the people we've known. Whoa, I can't imagine, for me, any other life being nearly as fulfilling and rewarding as that. It's incredible!

Through all of his ministry, the weddings, the funerals, the details, the joy, he said he got through it because he was never alone. I knew Dad had experienced extremes of emotion in doing his job and I asked him how he handled it:

Great question because there are so many emotional swings in a day. I can remember one day, I think it was in Hamburg, where I had a memorial service that was really tragic in the morning and then a wedding in the afternoon. That goes from a deep kind of sorrow and grief to absolute celebration and you've got to be fully present. You can't say, "I just did a funeral so I can't really celebrate your wedding," . . . you have to live that moment as fully as you can at that time. One of my challenges, probably both a strength and weakness in that regard, is that I'm very empathetic. If someone is hurting, my legs ache, I actually get a sympathetic pain in my legs. My point being in both those experiences, I'm really feeling what they are going through. [Then to] step out of that and come back and be real at home where those issues don't matter.

A good part of this transition is giving the burden of the day back to the Lord. It is a huge help to know ministry is doing God's work, not our work, and his promise to carry us along the way was a promise I claimed and experienced over and over again.

Dad finishes his devotion, "Worthiness," with a description that I think matched his life and work:

Paul is praying for us and when he comes to this part of his prayer he captures my attention in a fresh way. Three things in this prayer are gripping to me.

He prays that our lives are worthy of the Lord! Wow, what a great perspective for our lives! This reminds us that we do not "have to be good to become a Christian." Goodness is not a condition for being loved by God … it is a consequence! If we had to be "worthy" to be accepted by God we would all still be waiting out in the dark. God's love and grace come first and our desire for a life that is "worthy" of the Lord follows. This is a powerful motivation to being good people!

He prays for our good works. Being a Christian is not being saved for a comfortable relationship with the Lord. A Christian life involves our actions and good deeds for others. This means being more than moral in our personal lives ... language, habits, generosity, etc. ... but it also means caring for issues of peace and social justice in our community, nation and world.

He prays we may grow in the knowledge of God. I think it is instructive to see that this knowledge-factor comes after the works-factor because I think we know more of God's heart and will and power and grace when we have stepped out in doing good works for others in our world. We grow in understanding God through our obedience, our service, our ways of investing ourselves and our money in God's causes.

Paul's prayer makes me want to live a life that is "worthy" of the Lord who has saved me!

There was almost a too-good-to-be-true quality to Dad, as if no person could be that loving, supportive and lead a life that worthy of the Lord, as he describes in the devotion. There were times that he was so free with compliments that I almost didn't believe them, although they still made me feel good. On a card Mom and Dad gave me for my 45th birthday, there's a line drawing of a woman on the front. The card says, "Pretty Girl. Prettier Person." A friend joked that it seemed like something that would be given to a pre-teen struggling with self-image issues, but he was new to the charm of my parents.

Dad had a way, without uttering a word, of making you want to be a better person. He came to visit my office at my first real job out of college where I had a colleague, Ralph, who ceaselessly used profanity and also said he attended my dad's church. For the whole time

Dad was there, Ralph didn't utter a single curse word and my office-mate, Doug, said, "Can your dad come by every day?" This power reminded me of my mom's description of the grace she found from faith. Around my dad, you wanted to be a good person just because Dad was who he was, not because you had to earn his approval.

I think that influence came from the fact that he really was a good person, focused on others, trying to love everyone through "it," whatever their individual "it" was. But I also came to believe that was how he managed to keep his job fresh for forty years, by focusing on the individuals around him and what he could do to be of help. Instead of getting bored by having to write yet another sermon, which I imagine I would have felt by sermon number 500, definitely by sermon 1,000, and certainly by sermon 1,599, he seemed to defy that trend by relishing in the details and in people. After his death, Mom gave me his "quotes" file, to which he was still adding with things that inspired him all the way to the end of his life. One of his favorites in 2014 was a quote Mom gave him when she was reading *Americanah* by Chimamanda Ngozi Adichie, in which a character is described as "a person who did not have a normal spine but had, instead, a firm reed of goodness." Dad used the quote often to characterize the people that inspired him, unconscious of the fact that it described him to a tee.

FOURTEEN

Yearnings by Dick Leon, Daily Devotions, February 2009, Volume 36, Number 2, Northminster Presbyterian Church, Tucson, AZ

> As the deer pants for streams of water,
> so my soul pants for you, O God. Psalm 42:1

> I love the way the Bible drives us back to fundamental truths about life. In this Psalm, we are suddenly driven to ask ourselves this question: "What is the single, most essential ingredient for human beings to really be alive?"

WHAT DOES IT MEAN TO FULLY BE ALIVE? THAT WAS the heart of what I had been searching for. Meditating on teachings meant learning and seeing things differently, one of which was my dislike of asking for help. I like to be happy, independent and self-sufficient and so this entire journey had been a crack in my "I Know What I Am Doing" façade. My least favorite things to express would be: I am hurting, everything is not okay, I need help, and I have no clue what I'm doing or what my plan is. It felt as if I wore a carapace of assuredness that I had to remove in order to learn. Well, perhaps life cracked it open and then I crawled out and started to learn, and each time I found renewal, but also a tenderness that came with the continual admission that life is more than I can see. But what surprised me was that the journey left me feeling more vulnerable, a spiritual awareness of my small place in the mystery of life akin to the physical perspective that is apparent to me when I'm climbing.

By encouraging this humility and vulnerability, I was rewarded with new vitality and depth. The river of life was running deeper in me, turning laughter, which had always come easily to me, into delight, happiness into joy, concern into deep empathy, and trying into deeply caring about the outcome. Though sometimes the river ran closer to my surface than I expected. As Dad said at his retirement ceremony from Bellevue Presbyterian, "I feel as if my cup has runneth over and come out my eyes."

In 2011 I found myself sitting in the office of Steve, a small business development counselor explaining how I needed help to restructure a real estate loan. My husband, business partner and I had purchased a small commercial office building in late 2007 at the very top of the real estate market in Seattle. Even though our primary business partnership had broken apart in 2009, we still owned this building together in 2011 and its market value had dropped way below what we owed in mortgages. For many reasons, mostly geographical since my partners had moved on, I was in charge of administering the building, the loans, the cash flow, and the tenants. The numbers resulted in a net loss each month. I cleaned the building on Saturdays to cut expenses and was the person the tenants called when someone threw up outside the front door on a Sunday night, when the toilets ran endlessly, when rats appeared, and there were conflicts between tenants and even between their dogs.

News coverage at the time featured many stories of people just walking away from real estate that was under water, but despite one or both of my partners suggesting we do that, I found that I couldn't because it didn't seem honorable. I kept casting about for solutions. As a result, I ended up in Steve's office, meeting him for the first time and explaining how we had come to own this building and the difficult position it created at the end of every month. As I talked, the tears started rolling down my cheeks and I just pretended that they weren't there, completely embarrassed because I felt so unprofessional. Steve, who had a firm handshake, kind eyes and an avuncular presence, just let me continue and then explained all the things I needed to do in order to make a case for restructuring the loan. It was a long list of things that I inwardly groaned about: re-doing all the leases, modifying the operating agreement, changing the structure of the accounts, all things I didn't want to do and would take me a lot of time, time away from my primary business. But focusing on that list, the tears stopped and I finally managed to get out of Steve's office with some semblance of composure.

After I had chipped away at the list Steve had given me over several months I was sitting in his office again, reviewing each item and its result. There was a long pause after I finished my presentation, Steve looked at me, put his hand up to rub his chin, and said, "You know, not many people do the work on the lists that I give them so that they can turn a situation around."

I burst into tears again. Good grief, this river of Life was far too near the surface!! We hammered out a deal to restructure the loan over more years and at a lower interest rate so that I could keep the building running until we could finally sell it. Steve and I laughed about the tears and we ended up having a deeply authentic conversation about the tough situations in life.

Dad continually showed his vulnerability. He was confident and content but fully committed to exposing the depth of life. To me,

Dad always seemed so open, to learning, to admitting he was wrong, to finding out a new and better way to do things. In a sermon from 2010, he described his desire to be liked and to be positive:

> As a side note here, if you are feeling some tension between what Jesus is saying and what our culture teaches us to think about ourselves, how do you think I feel telling you this? I am constitutionally structured to want people to like me. When I graduated from High School all the seniors put their life goal in the yearbook; mine was "to have no enemies!" And now I'm saying what none of us want to hear: that we owe God more than we can ever pay! Is that a good idea? It is even funnier than that. I have a muscle condition that is being treated with prednisone and one of the side effects of prednisone is thin skin. So we have a people-pleasing preacher with thin skin telling all of you exactly what you don't want to hear!!

So why do this practice to face ourselves, expose our weaknesses and search for God and Truth? Dad answered this in the close of his devotion, "Yearnings:"

> This question is raised through the simple observation that the deer pants for streams of water in order to survive. Without water the deer cannot live. Water is an essential ingredient for life and so God created the deer with a built-in yearning for streams of water.
>
> Similarly, God created us with a built-in yearning that drives us to find one ingredient

above all others that will give us "life." Advertising agencies thrive on our inner restlessness so that we will buy their products. We are daily assaulted by promises of wealth, fame, happiness, good looks, sexual gratification, popularity, power, and a good night's sleep! All of these are good and appealing to us. But none of them relieves the one yearning that goes to the deepest core of our being so that we might indeed be fully alive: God.

Everything else is a masked substitute for a real and lasting relationship with God that will determine whether we are alive or dead! In the New Testament, there are three Greek words that are each translated "life" even though they mean something different. There is *bios* which means our physical life; there is *psyche* which means our emotional/mental life; and there is *zoe* which means our eternal life. Everyone has *bios* and *psyche*, but only those who put their trust in God by receiving Jesus Christ as Lord and Savior are given the gift we all yearn for the most: *zoe*, eternal life ... abundant life ... life that is in touch with the eternal!

Psalm 42 tells us that the deepest yearning of our soul is for God because God alone gives us the deepest and most lasting quality of being fully alive forever!

FIFTEEN

*13 Inches from God by Dick Leon, Daily Devotions,
December, 2012, Volume 38, Number 12,
Northminster Presbyterian Church, Tucson, AZ*

*They discussed it among themselves and said,
"If we say, 'From heaven,' he will ask, 'Why didn't you
believe him?' But if we say, 'Of human origin,' all the
people will stone us, because they are persuaded that
John was a prophet." So they answered, "We don't know
where it was from." Luke 2:5-8*

The religious leaders asked Jesus a question about
his authority and he asked them a question about John
the Baptist in return. They refused to answer because any answer
would get them in trouble. In other words, they
were **unwilling** to be honest and open with Jesus. And so,
Jesus refused to answer their question; he could see that
their hearts were not honestly open to him.

THERE ARE SEVERAL CANDLES THAT I LIGHT WHEN meditating at home. Over time, I have come to give them attributes or qualities that I want to cultivate: love, joy, character, courage, happiness, health, hope, faith, family and the one that I linger over longest, gratitude. For the first eighteen months of meditating, the list of things I was grateful for was along the lines of a backhanded-compliment—I'm grateful for the opportunities to see all my flaws clearly and work on them, I'm grateful that I've had the chance to get up after failing.

And then one day . . . it was simply gratitude for having a full, joyful heart. I sat down on the bolster and just basked in the contentment for several minutes. It felt like reaching the top of a mountain, when the relief and beauty combine to create a profound stillness. I was no longer alone, no longer hoping to have some faith, no longer practicing to have a spirit, but instead I was fully alive in the presence of the Divine. I had finally let the walls down so that I felt what had been there the whole time, something that is bigger than I am that has a toehold within me and is accessible in the quiet.

I had threaded a difficult needle to arrive at this conclusion. Choosing a spiritual practice that was more physical than my father's intellectual expression, reading and being inspired by many traditions and philosophies, I had walked a different path instead of following in his footsteps. Though I love and respect my parents so much—their presence, healthiness, selflessness—I needed to find a way that worked for me and to translate all that I had learned from my parents into a faith that I owned. In that moment when I realized my heart was full, I felt that faith coalesce from the pieces I had inherited from my parents; their values and the experience of forgiveness and grace combined with all the tools that I had been working on. I was doing what my dad had called stumble-proofing my life, letting the past and emotions go, quieting the inner voice and opening to a Divine presence. In this moment, at the peak of the spiritual mountain I had climbed, everything came together. I experienced something bigger that guides. I wasn't walking that path alone. By grace, I had been able to find my way there.

It is very difficult to verbalize this faith. Once my head is engaged to find the words, my self-doubt kicks in. Dad was so successful and revered in his life as a pastor, it's hard not to think that my way is less than his. He had such a defined and theological position and so I wonder if my love for any philosophy or tradition that inspires me is foolhardy. When Dad talked of the difficulty of a faithful life, I immediately question what I've experienced and conclude that it isn't hard enough so I must be missing something. When I think too much, I fear that what I believe will be found wanting next to the bright light that my dad shone for my whole life. Yet Dad's goal was to inspire people who believed and he has inspired me, so it is wrong, I know, to turn what I have done against myself by comparing myself to him.

Instead, I will trust this inner strength that I have discovered, remembering that it comes from something far greater than my own capabilities and will. I will enjoy a new type of confidence, not that all will always go well, but that I will be able to accept what happens and be open to how it will change my life for the better.

I found a line in a letter Dad wrote as a young man that summed up how I felt: "[I] know of an indomitable spirit and positivism that God somehow has laid within me."

Now, I ask myself the same question that I once asked about my father: what part in this new brand of confidence is attitude and discipline and what part does faith play? My attitude, which has naturally tended towards the optimistic and happy, has grown a new dimension, a gratitude for each and every day, even the sad ones. I find myself believing that instead of being stuck in a place because I believe I don't know how to move on from it, I will experience some days of grief and suffering, pain and doubt, but will lean in with this toolset that I've developed to understand and to accept life, beautiful and sad.

It takes discipline to sit down on the bolster every day regardless of my mood—happy, joyful, busy, distracted, grief-stricken. In that act, not knowing what I will find, I open myself up to discovery and learning, reading meditations and philosophies that often change that mood and widen my perspective. Simply complying with the act of trying, I force my ego and all that I thought I knew, wanted or feared to the back seat so that I have a chance of experiencing grace. For me, it feels as if the healing comes through my body and into my spirit. As if focusing on breathing, posture, and movement forces a perspective that tilts the way I see things until they click into a new, open position.

Starting in the fall of 2014, Deirdre moved our meditation class to a new studio so that we'd have more room. The new location was situated across the street from a new retail/residential high rise. This building replaced the old Carnation dairy factory in the Green Lake neighborhood and is about five stories high with a grocery store and a bank on the first floor and apartments or condos on the levels above and parking on the underground levels. Whether by design or oversight, the garbage dumpsters for this complex are contained within the building, not in an alley or on the street, so on Fridays, coincidentally at the same time as meditation class, every dumpster is attached to a small motorized vehicle that looks like a golf cart and dragged from underneath the building to a spot on the street where it is accessible to the garbage truck. On this particular Friday, as I was settling in, the garbage truck came, it attached its forks to the dumpsters and emptied each of the five dumpsters, creating a different clatter and by now, Deirdre was working hard to reframe the outdoor drama in terms of the people that were just doing their jobs. Did they have kids? Did they like their jobs? Was this particular dumpster location challenging for the garbage truck driver? And finally, when I was starting to get past this new auditory challenge, the empty dumpsters had to be dragged back by the motorized cart to their regular spots under the building.

The process filled the hour of our meditation. I was so irritated by the end I thought, "I don't need to go to class anymore." I had made it through my transformation, had healed my heart and established a spiritual practice that I could do on my own, and I couldn't see that signing up for dumpster aggravation on a weekly basis was good for my soul.

Nevertheless, I still signed up to continue the classes because I needed a toolset for ordinary life. Not every day can be spent summiting a mountain, but working out in preparation for the chance to climb is a daily occurrence. As far as mediation goes, I didn't want to go back to the days where I spent the majority of it focused on the pettiness of life where the biggest issues are the irritation of a neighbor that parks too close to my driveway, the sting of a comment made by a colleague, the fear that I might be facing unfairness, or the impatience of waiting for life to unfold. This is likely another piece I got from Dad, a desire not to focus on the worst that life has to offer but instead on the best. Once I figured out that was possible, I was determined to keep up the practice.

So, discipline kept me there until I discovered the patterns that feed my spirit and the goodness that I want to cultivate as a result of it. When I found my faith, I found that it felt like a boost. The boost that gets me over the hump when I'm afraid, the boost that sheds a little light when it's dark, the boost that allows me to see the extraordinary in the ordinary, the extra energy that makes hard things possible. No wonder Dad had so much enthusiasm. It feels like the boost my father always gave me, "You can do it, you are doing great. Be a servant, be useful, be open, loving and forgiving. Find whatever tools work to focus on those things …. life is beautiful indeed."

In the summer of 2009 my friend Doug and I took his daughter, Indigo, on a climb up Mt. Adams, a 12,276-foot peak in southeast Washington. Using a route on the south side of the mountain that isn't technical so no roping up is necessary, we hiked the first day with full packs, about 50 pounds, up to our base camp at about 9,000 feet. Doug and I carried heavy packs with the tent, sleeping bags, fuel, stove for boiling water, and individual equipment so that we didn't over-burden Indigo, who was 14 years old and carried plenty of weight, all of her individual equipment. It was her first climb and we wanted her to enjoy it as well as experience it.

After reaching the Lunch Counter, the spot for our base camp and setting up the tent, we made dinner (instant noodle packets of fettuccini with broccoli and chicken in a cream sauce), drinks (tea, cocoa or cider) consumed in the same cup, a climbing trick to help lighten the load, and then boiled water to refill our drinking water supply. Sitting around our stove, we told stories of other climbs, like the last time we summitted Adams in 2001, the outhouse precariously perched on the side of a cliff at 13,000 feet on Mt. Elbrus, and the time we celebrated my birthday on a climb of Rainier and all of my fellow climbers were asleep by 7:30pm. We talked about the route we'd take up, Doug having a perfect memory of all the features of the route from the last time, and Indigo seeming delighted to be with her dad on this adventure.

We settled into our sleeping bags after watching the first stars come out on this clear night at the end of June and set our alarms for 2 A.M. Our goal was to be climbing by 3 A.M. after getting our gear on, eating breakfast (oatmeal), and having a hot drink (same cup), so that we could climb when the snow was still hard and also have time to get back down to our base camp, pack up, hike out to the car and drive the five hours home all in one day.

The first part out of camp was a steep snowfield, almost 50 degrees, up to a false summit at 11,000 feet. We climbed the first couple hours in silence and dark, the few steps ahead illuminated by the circular glow of our headlamps as we zigzagged back and forth to create our own switchbacks because it was too steep to go straight up. As the combination of the effort, fifty steps to gain ten or so vertical feet, thin air and fatigue set in, I started to doubt that it was worth it. "I'm tired. I've done this before. I'm cold. I didn't work out enough." There were too many doubts to count and too much time to consider each one. But then the sky started to lighten and, wow, to the south Mt. Hood became visible, so I believed I could take 500 more steps. Then we took a break to drink water and don our sunglasses and Indigo had a huge smile on her face and I could take 500 more steps. Each revelation brought a boost and made each hard step possible until five hours after we'd left base camp, we were standing on the summit. Indigo, who didn't utter a single complaint, bundled in her down jacket, was simply radiant, Doug beamed with pride at his daughter, and as we looked out at Rainier, Mt. St. Helens, and into Oregon – Hood, Jefferson, possibly even the Three Sisters—we knew each step was worth it. It was truly extraordinary and every fear, tired thought, and the darkness of the night were wiped out. By God, we made it!

Finding my faith feels as if I am at the glorious summit of a mountain every day. I can access the extraordinary just by walking Biscuit. I'm awake to the joy of climbing the thirty-foot hill right by my house, am energized by the smile of a stranger as we talk briefly on the street, and exult in the sunrises over Green Lake. Each dark morning is filled with the beautiful potential of revelation.

Dad finishes his devotion, "13 Inches from God," with his favorite quote from Blaise Pascal:

> When we see people who say they "cannot believe in God, or Jesus, or the church, or the Christian faith" … however they may put it … we need to know that at least a part of the problem is not one of "cannot" but rather of "will not!"
>
> Coming to faith in Jesus is deeper than a matter of the head. It is always a matter of **the heart first**. It is the heart that leads us to faith more than the head, will more than intellect, an open and willing spirit more than reason. My good friend Blaise Pascal's most famous line goes like this:
>
> *"The Heart has its reasons,*
> *that reason does not know."*
>
> The distance between our heart and our head is about 13 inches. When our hearts are right our heads will follow along by believing. That 13 inches is just how far most unbelievers are from finding God, or, better yet, letting God find them.

I read the words Dad has written and know that I've studied the same sentiment many times in a mediation. Mark Nepo brings together quotes from Lao-Tzu, the founder of Taoism, a yoga practice, and a story of a Gregorian nun in his meditation, "A Profound Bow:"

All streams flow to the sea
Because it is lower than they are,
Humility gives it its power.
– Lao-Tzu

There is a Yoga mudra, a kneeling posture of exercise, where by bringing your head to your chest while extending your arms up and out behind you, you can practice placing your head beneath your heart. And from this humbling position, you can't help but tire, and so, you must put your arms down. With your head beneath your heart, you must stop doing.

Soon after learning this, I came upon a woman who had been a nun, and she told me that she would practice for days upon days similar postures of Gregorian Chant: incline, bow and profound bow – each bringing the head lower and lower to the earth.

This holds a powerful lesson: Time and time again, the head must be brought beneath the heart or the ego swells. If you do not bend, life will bend you. In this way, humility is accepting that your head belongs beneath your heart, with your thinking subordinate to your feeling, with your will subordinate to the higher order. This acceptance is key to receiving grace.

Lay your head down and the world of being will open its joys.

Do any two people actually believe exactly the same thing? Instead of focusing on the differences, I can see the beautiful patterns that connect us. I feel the grace of God working within me and bow my head and experience the joy.

SIXTEEN

The Beautiful Life by Dick Leon, Daily Devotions,
January 2012, Volume 39, Number 1,
Northminster Presbyterian Church, Tucson, AZ

But the fruit of the Spirit is love, joy, peace, forbearance, kindness, goodness, faithfulness, gentleness and self-control. Against such things there is no law. Galatians 5:22-23

DAD LET ME ASK QUESTION AFTER QUESTION AND WAS so open that I think he must not have had any sour spots in his life memory. His eyes lit up and his smile was infectious, "These conversations get me to reflect back to figure out who I am, and why I am who I am, and I love the exercise of it all."

He was so well integrated by the end of his life that the separate threads of attitude, discipline and faith braided tightly together for him. He was always upbeat. Even when he was worried about something, he was upbeat, just with a little worry on the side. The most remarkable part of his attitude, I have come to see, was enthusiasm. I have learned that enthusiasm translates from the Greek word *en-theos* to "*In* God."

Three years before he died, on one of my visits to Tucson, my mom and I were in the living room and Dad yelled to us from his study, "Isn't the sunrise beautiful this morning? We are so lucky."

And Mom yelled back, "Dick, it's absolutely wonderful!"

I could see my mom wasn't really paying attention and said to her in a low tone, "It's okay, Mom, I won't tell him you didn't even look."

Mom replied, "He can't even see the sunrise from where he's sitting."

Dad created his own sunshine. From talking with Aunt Margie, Uncle Russ and friends from his youth, I know that this was always characteristic of Dad. With his faith came a direction for this enthusiasm, a way of channeling it towards service to others.

Since his death, I have gone back to the materials he left and I'm drawn over and over again to his time in India. It was such a formative time for him, far from his everyday life, and he was young enough to still be establishing the patterns and disciplines that would carry him through life. In addition, he traveled a lot within India during school breaks so his letters show the maturity and discipline growing within him. He wrote:

> My Bible study was shot during our travels and ever since returning I've nearly left it altogether, my prayers have become irregular, undisciplined and superficial and thus my days have become likewise. I'm beginning to think that as one prays so will he live; if superficially, then so in life, if deeply introspective, then so in life; if intensely personal and loving, then so in life.

In that description, I find so much similarity to what I've determined for my own spiritual practice. For all the years that I didn't meditate or have any spiritual practice at all, I had a more superficial life. Everything went along just fine for quite some time but it lacked depth and meaning, the type of purpose that gives a texture to my days regardless of the tasks I am focused on. Dad said, "We need help from outside ourselves when looking for Life and Truth."

So Dad's discipline and focus were centered on the message that he drew from the Bible and the person of Jesus. Dad stated the list of the disciplines for me many times in our conversations and they differed slightly in wording from time to time but always it was love, forgiveness, servanthood, humility: "Love your enemies, forgive 70x70 times, to be great we must be servant of all, deny yourself and take up His cross of servanthood, He came not to be served but to serve and no disciple is greater than his master, God has brought His Kingdom or rule to this world through Him."

And faith? I was surprised to discover that I didn't ask him that question as directly as I thought I had, given that I was so intent on it. But as I dug through all the materials I have from him, I've concluded that I think faith for Dad was obedience. It's a word he uses over and over to describe his path. Dad's journey, coming to his faith because of the truthfulness of what he saw in Jesus Christ, seems so intellectual to me and maybe that is because it requires putting faith into words to transfer the knowledge from him to me. But he confirmed his journey had been very cerebral overall and then described how it all hung together for him:

> There have been deep, emotional experiences along the way but the primary thing that happened to me was when I came to the conclusion that Jesus Christ was true and I could trust Him with what He said, and He could be the one who would show me how to live, then I said, "Okay, I'm going to follow that."

In the months after Dad's death, as I was trying to put it all together, it was Mom who finally provided the answer I was looking for about faith. As always, it was far easier to get a definitive answer from her. She said that it was by faith that Dad set the path of his life and by faith that he stayed on that path even when he wasn't sure what it would bring. He explained to me in our conversations that it didn't happen all at once for him either, but was validated as he lived out his commitment:

> I know now that I also had to be open, in my heart, to want to follow Christ, but it was the decision-making that made it happen. The other side of the story is that as I lived out that conviction of following Christ and being obedient to Christ, life's gone well. I mean life isn't without trouble, there has been plenty of trouble, but I look back at life and had I not become a Christian and followed Christ, who knows what I would have done.

After about three months of studying in India, Dad wrote about the religious and cultural discussions he was having with other students at Benares Hindu University. It was clear he was working through the best way to have a dialogue with many people who were willing to be very candid and verbose about their beliefs. It was good, he said, "So long as I don't turn it into a debate where we become more firmly entrenched in our own prejudices. So, I've tried to become the student and interested listener, which I am, and let them talk on." Almost fifty-five years later, Dad was still a student and interested listener as he and I talked about faith, spiritual practice and family. I asked him if he was sure he was right about his beliefs. He replied,

Of the core issues I am. I've come now to call myself a big tent guy. I think there are people of faith from all walks who see in Jesus what God has shown—that there is no one else like him with his quality of love, wisdom and self-sacrifice.

In a way I have become less cocky or confident because I thought I had things all figured out early on, but now I know I have general things figured out, but the fact is that we differ in this huge tent of the family of faith on different things.

[For example] there are people who for many reasons, historically or culturally perhaps, can't focus on Jesus. But the God we know through Jesus is that same God that made everyone and is doing all he can, I believe, to reach out, regardless of background. I believe there is something else, heaven, which translates as God's space and that God has loved all the world enough to come down and die for our sins. Is that the kind of God that would say, "If you don't spell my name right, you are not in?" That doesn't fit the character of God. I don't know how or the way he will do it, but I certainly trust God to make those decisions generously, fairly, with mercy and love.

I've thought this often about you and your world with all the disciplines that are so wonderfully therapeutic. It seems to me that Christ is equally as present and could be equally named and known to you. The disciplines in a sense are more along the horizontal level than perhaps the

> vertical level (reaching up to God) and Christ honors anything that makes us more what God wants us to be.
>
> I am thrilled with what is happening in you in this journey and one of the great benefits is that it brings us closer. When kids follow in a trail similar to their parents, it creates one more way they can be close and can relate with each other ... and in this case relate deeply and lastingly.

Dad never managed to have that conversation of faith with his own father. Dad was only 38 when his dad died at age 63.

Our first visit back to the States when living in the Philippines was in the summer of 1972. We saw our extended families and I got my first glimpse of snow. In that year my dad's father, Bumpa to his grandchildren, was diagnosed with Amyotrophic Lateral Sclerosis (ALS), or Lou Gehrig's disease. He was still young, in his 60's, when he suffered the first signs of the illness. He had a little VW bug and as he drove out to one of the offices for Washington Title, he had to stop along the road because his arms were so tired from holding the steering wheel; he couldn't even crank up the window.

The doctor said that Doug's personality would change, he'd get angry, cranky and mean-spirited but Dad said he never did. He was always very gentle and considerate.

Dad went home again to visit in 1973 when Bumpa was still mobile but no longer working. Dad was hoping to talk with him about matters of faith, to have a substantive conversation for once, but he remembered:

> He just never was good at doing that. There was no evidence of fear or openness to talk about death. He was more determined to assure all of us

by saying "It'll be fine" and "we'll work through it." He just was a very upbeat, positive guy and he was not going to mope about it. There was a touch of unreality but again it was an upbeat and positive spirit. We all face death and grief and loss differently, and for my dad it was a matter of being courageous and thoughtful of my mom and the rest of the family.

During our conversations Dad suggested that faith, or the expression of it, differs by generation. Perhaps his generation was more concerned with the issue that drove him – truthfulness—and my generation is more concerned with political correctness and inclusiveness.

In their book *Generations: The History of America's Future, 1584 to 2069,* published in 1992, William Strauss & Neil Howe track the 18 American generations from 1584 to the present and then make predictions for generations to come. In their findings they posit that there are four different generational types and that they progress in the same pattern throughout our history oscillating between two different types of social movements: secular crises, which focus on outer world institutions and public behavior, and spiritual awakenings, which focus on inner world or values and behavior. They describe the general experience for each type.

My generation, the Generation X (called the 13ers in the book), is what they call the reactive type: "...individualism flourishes, new ideals are cultivated in separate camps, confidence in institutions declines, and secular problems are deferred."

In contrast, they describe my parents' generation, the Silent Ones, as the adaptive type: "Society turns toward conformity and stability, triumphant ideals are secularized and spiritual discontent is deferred."

So Dad's theory about the expression of faith being different for each generation can be explained sociologically. Each generation reacts to how they were raised and it affects how they parent and participate in society but in a predictable way, so as we make what we think are individual choices, we really are participating in waves of secularism and spiritualism, individualism and public action. But as our discussions proceeded, I began to see the similarities more than the differences as we talked about how faith played out in his life and mine. It's a tool set of prayers/meditation, confession, forgiveness, inspiration and guidance to help set boundaries so that you don't get into trouble, to heal when you are suffering, and to inspire when things get boring.

Dad's doctoral thesis was on sickness and healing. As a pastor, the issue of healing, working with people who are sick, hurting and broken was a big part of his job. Praying for healing, visiting people in the hospital, he dealt with death and dying almost daily. He wanted to study whether there was a relationship between sin and sickness as well as between faith and healing. The extreme position, the fringe right that he saw when we were in the Philippines, was a movement that claimed healing powers and signs of wonder, whereas, most in mainline Christianity don't want to touch that because of so many abuses that arise from false promises. Dad wanted to address the issue of faith, healing, sickness and sin from the middle viewpoint, from the Reformed Tradition rather than the fringe right.

He tackled the connections between sin and sickness and healing and faith. The example he gave me was that some people say that sickness is always a sign of sin so if you confess your sin, you will be healed. Or others will say that healing always happens if you have enough faith. In his thesis Dad drew the conclusion that there is no simple relationship between sin and sickness or between faith and healing. If someone got drunk and drove 100 mph down the highway and had an accident, it seems clear that there is a causal relationship in that accident. But, if a six-year-old comes down with cancer in her leg, he thought it would be terrible to attribute that to a sin, adding a sense of guilt that should not be there on top of the sickness.

Instead of a direct relationship between healing and faith, he found the many healing therapies of God that come through faith: prayer, hymns, and worship services that bring people back to their spiritual center. It seemed that Dad's list was any practice that changes the focus to God, not the individual. Dad believed the whole Christian life was about healing – healing our relationship with God and healing our relationship with others. Dad also included modern medicine as a healing therapy of God, believing that it works hand in hand with spiritual practices:

> One other development that helped me describe healing was when modern medicine discovered the deep relationship between mind and body so that some illnesses were termed psychosomatic. There used to be a huge separation between spiritual things and medicine, but in this last century medicine has come to recognize that a person's spirit – their attitude, their mindset, their faith, what they believe in, what they are scared of – has a huge impact on their body. The Christian faith has always understood the interplay between the body and the spirit by having a holistic understanding of the human personality. I used to kid people when talking about the

soul and the little phrase I came up with is: "You don't *have* a soul according to the Bible. No, the Bible would say you *ARE* a soul!" The soul is not something separate in you; you are a whole being, body, mind and spirit, all of that is who you are and it is all interrelated.

Dad finished his devotion, "The Beautiful Life," with a list of what he sees as the results of living a life of faith.

I think I am right in remembering that John Adams, our second President, once said, "Freedom cannot survive without religious faith." His point was that freedom requires an inner restraint to bad behavior. Soft governments (in contrast to police states) cannot compel good behavior; they can only impose penalties for wrong-doing. Only faith moves us to be good. (Sadly, as faith dwindles in our society more oppressive Laws are needed to rein us in!)

Paul, in his letter to Galatia, is saying the same thing. In Christ we are now free from living under the Law (outside us). Now we are to live by the Spirit (inside us). It is the Spirit that makes life beautiful inside and out.

Consider these fruits of the Spirit in our life that come when we follow Christ:
- Love—the mature kind of love that chooses to be loving
- Joy—that is deeper and more enduring than happiness

- Peace—not the absence of conflict but the presence of God
- Forbearance—the strength to carry on regardless
- Kindness—the gift of genuine caring for other people
- Goodness—the quality that shines in Christian living
- Faithfulness—being trustworthy people to those around us
- Gentleness—the strength to show our soft side to others
- Self-control—the power to tame destructive impulses!

No Law can generate that kind of behavior in our lives. But when Christ makes His home in our heart and the Holy Spirit sets up shop in our lives, then these are going to be the marks of a wholesome, joyous, generous, beautiful life!

Dad's devotion could include one more point that he knew well: faith also cannot be compelled. My parents could set the example, show us what a good life is and wish faith for us, but we all have to find our own way there.

As we talked about his life stories and journeys and all that we shared, there was one question I wasn't sure if I was brave enough to ask. I loved my gentle father so much that his answer could break my heart. I knew how much he had given me without asking for anything in return and that pride in me as a good kid, good daughter, who somehow survived to this point regardless of how many times I hadn't been, to my mind, could be at stake. But because I had gotten so much more confident that I could handle the full depth of life, good or bad, I was able to ask.

"Has it, in any way, taken away from your life and accomplishments that your children haven't followed in your faith's footsteps?" Dad answered:

> The most important thing for me is that each of you come to experience and love God in your own way. We are all children of God and God is larger and more mysterious than any one of us can imagine. But life has been so rich for me because of what I have come to know of God through Jesus that on that level I yearn for you to know the same deep contentment and certainty that you belong to God and God loves you.

This last question, the one that gets to the heart of what I always feared which is that my behavior or beliefs would impact his job and faith, is the one I am most glad I asked and I cherish my dad's answer. He had as always made me feel loved. I knew ever more deeply that he was proud of me. I felt an active and present sense of God as he worked through Dad.

SEVENTEEN
JUNE, 2015

"To truly listen is to risk being changed forever."

- Sa'k'ej Henderson, Native American Elder
(From Book of Awakening, Mark Nepo*)*

DURING MY THIRTIES, I WAS MARRIED BUT MOSTLY learning about what not to do. All that I was learning through meditation about living a more meaningful and purposeful life, as well as spending time with my beautiful parents was a blessing for my early forties, but I reached a pivotal jumping off point as I approached my 45th birthday. I knew that I would really regret not having a family, in part from understanding my legacy better, in part from having the blessing of being involved with my brother's kids as they were growing up, and mostly because I had happy and successful friends who regretted that they didn't have kids when they had the chance.

    I was open to joining a family that was already in progress, but I didn't find either a partner with one or one with the toolset that matched the one I'd developed. Out to dinner to celebrate my birthday with my dear friends, Sue and Jill, I said that I wanted a family of my own. By stating it out loud, I pushed myself into action. They told me I had better get on it. I had run out of time to do it the old-fashioned way.

I told my brother, Jay, and his wife, Lindsey, that I was thinking of in-vitro fertilization and they both were ecstatic, telling me that they supported me 100% and we'd all be in this together. Jay, who has raised two beautiful and vibrant daughters, Sarina and Claire, has so much of my father in him. Throughout the challenges of life, Jay has held the same attitude that Dad had, focusing on the positive and taking the high road. So I couldn't have been luckier, knowing he was completely onboard as the male role model in my baby's life. I stopped telling people lest I hear a different opinion and got busy making the many decisions. I winnowed down the potential donors and then Jay, Lindsey, Jill, Sue, and I voted on them, amazingly all in agreement. A completely different way to get pregnant—by committee. With great medical advice and guidance, I was pregnant within six months of that 45th birthday dinner.

It was Jay who first felt the impact of Dad's dying without knowing about my plans. He driven all night from San Francisco to Tucson and in the quiet moments along dark roads, Jay, as a father himself, felt a deep sadness that Dad died not knowing of one more grandchild to come. I had thought I had so much time, that it would be better to tell the family after the in-vitro worked, if it worked, but needless to say, I didn't wait any longer and told Mom when we were all together the day after Dad's death. She was incredibly supportive as well. One of Dad's closest friends is a retired fertility specialist and there were several funny moments that week as we were all together having dinner and Barry was telling stories, completely unbidden by us, about people who already had kids becoming pregnant with twins or triplets. When I went in for the embryo transplant with Lindsey accompanying me, the specialist recommended implanting just one embryo, and I agreed to that plan without hesitation. I finally did tell Barry that I was pregnant and that he totally had freaked me out with his stories of multiple births!

I reflect on the fact that just as I am about to become a single mom, my mom has become a single mom, albeit of adult children. And as I enter this phase without a father, I'm bringing a little girl into this world without a father. But there is Jay and the rich tapestry of family and faith to build upon.

If I have overlooked anything in this account of finding my father's faith, it is the very real tie that Mom brought to the table. She was there for all our conversations and walks and provides, when I need it, the link between Dad's idealism and the practical application of faith. After Dad's death as my mother works through her grief and all of us kids with our own, the temptation is to have an ongoing chorus of Dad, Dad, Dad. But in the sweet melody that ties us together through it all, I find Mom's voice so singular and strong. Enthusiasm was the word for Dad. Grace is the word for Mom.

Grace is such a quiet characteristic, loving and warm, and it complimented Dad's enthusiasm so perfectly. I wasn't completely aware it was there until she started to fly solo. Mom's grace has a constancy and strength all of its own. It guided Mom's actions throughout the funerals and is now visible as she already takes care of me and my unborn child. This little girl is so lucky to be born into this grief-stricken but not fractured family.

My dad wrote me an email after I sent him an early draft of this manuscript:

> Thank you so much, dear Wynne, for even thinking of doing this … let alone giving it such a

> good start. You know what this reminds me of … how when you were little I would hold you close, face to face, knock on your forehead and ask if anyone is home … and we'd laugh and laugh together. The picture of the two of us that we blew up in that pose always made me feel that closeness all over again, and this 'project' of yours does that same thing!

I feel this closeness to him even now. Of course, I wish that he knew about my baby daughter, that he was there for the news and the pregnancy, but it doesn't stop there because I will want him there for all the holy moments ahead, birth, baptism, marriage (if I find the right life partner even after doing this backwards). I wish my little girl could know him as I did, but in the saddest moments, I am comforted that I finally do have faith, that I can feel him near because of that and so he's with me. And I know what he's saying, "It's going to be great, kid. You're doing great."

Dick and Wynne, 1971

Acknowledgments

THERE ARE TWO PEOPLE, IN ADDITION TO MY DAD, without whom this book simply would never have been written. Carolyn Vandiver Leon, my mom, and Sheila Bender, my writing coach.

My dad was a good man. He worked at it and he surrounded himself with people that made him a better person, most notably, my mom. A lot of his earthly strength came from her. She has amazing courage and wisdom and has always been willing to cover home base. She has played that same role for me in this process. When I thought writing this was too risky, too boring, or too hard, knowing that Mom was with me kept me going. Whereas Dad was a deductive thinker, seeing the big picture and racing forward, Mom is an inductive thinker, pulling all the pieces together. Her talent as an editor is evident on each page of this book.

Sheila Bender listened, encouraged and cajoled a narrative at a time when all that ran through my head and heart was a single mantra—I love my daddy and I miss him. Her willingness to play the role of the hungry reader created a vortex into which I could write, and her encouragement and wisdom kept me wanting to do better.

Dr. Scott Dudley, Senior Pastor of Bellevue Presbyterian Church, played the role that I would have asked my father to do, providing feedback as a pastor. He, like Dad, was gentle and encouraged me as Dad encouraged him.

Dr. Andy Ross, Senior Pastor of Northminster Presbyterian Church in Tucson, Arizona, graciously allowed me to use the devotions that Dad wrote for Northminster and was his ebullient self in his excitement for the project.

I got the first line of this book from my dear friend, Melinda Layman Smith. Thank you for that and for 20 years of friendship, wisdom and laughter. I am so grateful for the encouragement of all my wonderful friends that were early readers and supporters of this project. Your interest, support and friendship mean even more than the feedback because that is essentially what helped guide me to the finish line.

I am thankful to my family for giving me the latitude to express my journey and thoughts in this memoir even though we all have unique viewpoints from which we see Dad.

I have been lucky enough to be loved by the four communities of faith where my dad served as pastor. In Spokane, not only was I taken in by the Williams and Shoemakers when my parents had to depart for Bellevue Presbyterian Church, but I spent most of my growing up years being guided, loved and supported by all the wonderful friends and families that were part of an amazing community.

To all my friends from meditation class, thank you for pulling me along in the slipstream of growth and enlightenment. I feel like I'm in a gentle circle of wise women when I sit down to meditate with you and it always makes me a better person.

Book List

THERE ARE MANY BOOKS THAT I PORED OVER IN TRYing to shape this book and my spiritual practice. Here are the ones mentioned in this narrative. For more resources, devotions and pictures, please visit http://www.findingmyfathersfaith.com

Adichie, Chimamanda Ngozi. *Americanah* (Anchor Books, 2013).

Chödrön, Pema. *How to Meditate* (Sounds True, 2013).

Chödrön, Pema. *Living Beautifully with Uncertainty and Change* (Shambala Publications, 2013).

Chödrön, Pema. *When Things Fall Apart* (Shambala, 2010).

Nepo, Mark. *The Book of Awakening* (Conari Press, 2000).

Ortberg, John. *Know Doubt* (Zondervan, 2008).

Peck, M. Scott. *Further Along the Road Less Traveled* (Touchstone Press, 1993).

Strauss, William and Howe, Neil. *Generations: The History of America's Future, 1584 to 2069* (Harper Perennial, 1991).

Tariri with Wallis, Ethel Emily. *Tariri My Story* (Harper & Row, 1965).

Taylor, Jill Bolte. *My Stroke of Insight* (Plume, 2009).

About the Author

WYNNE LEON IS A BUSINESS OWNER SPECIALIZING IN helping corporations collaborate through the use of web technologies. She holds a bachelor's of science degree in electrical engineering from the University of Washington.

Leon is also the coauthor of two technical books, *Implementing Exchange Server* and the *Microsoft SharePoint Server 2007 Bible*.

An enthusiast of endurance adventures, Leon is an amateur mountain climber and a mom.

Made in the USA
Charleston, SC
26 May 2016